Greek Oranges

To Arvid C. Swanston
*a long-time friend and
a man with a proper
appreciation of the
classic dessert*

ACKNOWLEDGMENTS

Desserts prepared for photography by Marie Kason
of WILTON ENTERPRISES, INC.
and by LOUIS SZATHMARY ASSOCIATES
under the supervision of Louis I. Szathmary.
Photography by Edward Hois.

THE WILTON BOOK OF CLASSIC DESSERTS

EDITED BY EUGENE AND MARILYNN SULLIVAN

PUBLISHED BY

PINE TREE PRESS
CHICAGO

WILTON ENTERPRISES, INC., 833 WEST 115TH STREET, CHICAGO 60643

INTRODUCTION

During the past three or four centuries, desserts have passed through a "golden age." Imaginative chefs of many nationalities have brought great artistic talents to bear in creating classic finales to distinguished meals.

At the height of this "golden age," pastry cooks took precedence over musicians, sculptors and other artists. As a result, the dessert took on the character of an art form. Carême, "the Cook of kings and the King of cooks," expressed a point of view 150 years ago that true dessert lovers accept today: 'the fine arts are five in number, to wit: painting, sculpture, poetry, music and architecture—whose main branch is confectionery.'

Many of the desserts that have become *classic* were created to render appropriate honor to victorious admirals, celebrated opera stars, reigning monarchs, revered saints, national institutions and assorted events considered to be of monumental importance. Others had more humble origins. *All* have lived!

Most of my long-time favorite recipes, of course, are also the favorites of generations of pastry fanciers, dedicated "tasters" who would never consider any meal very worthwhile, if the all-important final touch did not appear in the form of some noteworthy sweet.

Here we have assembled a generous sampling of the most famous classic desserts, all of which you can prepare in your own kitchen. Original recipes have been followed as closely as possible, with no short-cuts included. Some of these are quite easily made. Others must be created at the more unhurried tempo of the old world. Take the little extra time and care to be artistic. The results are worth it.

NORMAN WILTON

CONTENTS

FOREWORD

The most important job for a chef or for a housewife is the menu planning and the most important parts of the menu are the first and the very last things on it.

If a family and its guests or the customers of a restaurant sit down to a meal, their very first and very last impressions will be the most important. It is a theory, according to which remembering things is a reverse program. We remember first what happened last and we are "rolling up" the memory of the event backwards. This is why I feel dessert is so important.

The Wilton book of Classic Desserts, in my opinion, is one of the best I ever encountered and I have (among my over 4,000 cookbooks) a very large number on desserts and sweets alone.

The most significant characteristic of this book, in my opinion, is the fact that it gives a generous sampling of time-tested, widely accepted classic desserts, many of them created by famous chefs; others by unknown but very talented housewives all over the world. But, they have one thing in common: they are all real recipes with real ingredients, without shortcuts, substitutes and compromises.

An eating experience to be joyful and as perfect as possible must involve all our senses. The enjoyment of food is not the joy of the tastebuds alone. By far not! The shape and color of the food is a joy to the eyes. So is the way it is presented.

The smell and aroma of the food is a joy to the nostrils.

Its texture, consistency, temperature is a joy for our sense of touch.

Its crunchy, snapping, crispness, crustiness, is a joy to our ears and, of course, its taste, its consistency, its chewing quality and mouthfeel to our tastebuds.

Therefore, it is very important that a homemaker as a menu planner should plan the menu carefully to mix and match shapes, colors, sauces, consistencies, temperatures, textures, not to make the meal monotonous.

The dessert can give new color sensations, additional textures, additional temperatures to the main course of the meal. After a smooth and creamy chicken a la king, a *croquembouche;* after a pot roast served with a Van Dyke brown gravy and vivid green string beans, *"oranges à la grecque,"* the beautiful crimson syrup slowly dribbling down on translucent peeled oranges accented with the faint bitterness and chewiness of julienned orange rind—what a delightful contrast!

After the selection of the proper dessert, it is very important to be sure that all the needed ingredients and utensils, tools, containers are on hand before we start. If we feel that it will take us an hour to do it we should allow ourselves two hours to be sure that we won't run out of time.

Housewives should never try something which they never tried before when they expect important guests. Experimenting and entertaining don't go well together, and the homemaker should rather shine with a very simple and often tried dessert than be embarrassed with a great artistic undertaking resulting in a flop.

Last, but not least, the selection of the serving dish. The way of presentation of the dessert is of utmost importance. The most elegant and best prepared food can turn into an insignificant thing if not presented properly.

A clean doily, a few fresh green leaves from the garden, an extra sprinkling of powdered sugar, a few candied flowers, some freshly grated chocolate are as important for the dessert as lipstick for the homemaker.

The tools are also important. A dull improper knife can ruin a beautiful cake and certain desserts served without the tools designated for their serving can make guests very unhappy.

Well chosen ingredients, good equipment, excellent tools, patience, and before anything else, the love of cooking, the zest of life and the spirit of undertaking, together with this book will help the housewife to create memorable classic desserts.

CHEF LOUIS SZATHMARY

Mr. Szathmary was educated as a journalist and psychologist in his native Hungary. He has been actor, soldier, marriage counselor, prisoner of war, lecturer and most importantly, chef. He serves as food consultant to industry, and operates The Bakery, a truly fine Chicago restaurant.

Sonntags Haselnusstorte

GÂTEAUX DE GRANDES FÊTES

Cakes for Big Celebrations

Here is a sampling of classic pastries on an international scale—the ingratiating *dolci* of Italy, the deliciously refined and artistic *gateaux* of France, the baroque, schlag-bedecked *torten* of the cities of the Danube, and the substantial sweets of England. These masterpieces represent the peak of the *patissier's* art, "cakes for big celebrations." They reflect the charm and color of a romantic era when the appearance of a dessert was just as important as its unsurpassed flavor.

Their preparation requires planning and attention to detail, but the really essential ingredients are the love and care it takes to create a spectacular climax to an important occasion. The appreciation of your guests and your own satisfaction in taking part in a centuries-old art will be ample reward for your efforts.

Many of these desserts are based on a few classic mixtures—pâtè à chou, génoise, meringue Suisse, puff paste—all found in Chapter VII. Once these fundamentals are mastered, the production of these timeless favorites becomes quite simple. The final touches of icings, fillings and sauces are in Chapter VIII.

SOME *people look ahead to the last chapter to make sure the books ends happily. Others ask what there is for dessert before beginning dinner.*

GÂTEAU GRANDE FÊTE

A marvelous confection from Switzerland perfumed with raspberries and cognac. It should be prepared a day or so in advance to mellow and blend flavors.

> 1 9″ Almond Cake (Chapter VII)
> ¼ cup cognac
> 1 recipe Swiss broyage (Chapter VII)
> 1 cup raspberry jam
> 1 recipe Continental Butter Cream, chocolate flavored (Chapter VIII)
> 1 cup toasted blanched slivered almonds
> Confectioners' sugar for dusting

Sprinkle the almond cake with the cognac and let it stand for half an hour.

Bake the broyage in 2 thin 9″ layers. Place one layer on a serving plate and spread with half of the jam. Place Almond Cake on top, spread with remaining jam and top with second Broyage layer.

Reserve one-half cup of the Chocolate Butter Cream. Ice the sides of the cake with the remainder, and press the almonds into the iced sides. Pipe a border of rosettes around the top of the cake with the reserved Butter Cream. Dust top with sifted confectioners' sugar.

SACHERTORTE

So famous is this cake that the original recipe for it was the subject of a law suit that lasted for seven years in the courts of Vienna. The Sacher Hotel, run by the descendants of Chef Franz Sacher, who invented the torte for Prince Metternich in 1832, claimed that its version was the only one entitled to bear the name "the original Sachertorte". This was countered by Demel's, the famous pastry shop, declaring Demel's had purchased from Franz's grandson, Edouard Sacher, the right to etch the "genuine Sachertorte" seal in the purest bittersweet on the Demel's product alone. Demel's version is covered with apricot glaze, then iced in chocolate. The Sacher's is a two-layer cake filled with apricot jam.

The court finally decided in the hotel's favor, but controversy still rages in the Sacher's dignified coffee room, the baroque halls of Demel's and wherever pastry-lovers gather. On one point there is total agreement: Sachertorte is even finer with whipped cream served on the side.

Here is a version of Sachertorte, not necessarily authentic, but very good.

A CAKE *should be a treat to the eye and the palate.*

> ¾ cup butter
> ¾ cup sugar
> 6 eggs, separated
> 1 teaspoon vanilla
> 6 ounces semi-sweet chocolate, melted
>   and cooled
> 2 cups sifted flour
> 1 recipe Apricot Glaze (Chapter VIII)
> 1½ cups Chocolate Fondant (Chapter VIII)

Cream the butter till fluffy, slowly add the sugar and beat till well blended. Add the egg yolks, one at a time, beating after each addition.

Whip the egg whites until stiff and gently fold the chocolate into them. Combine the two mixtures and carefully fold in the flour until just blended. Do not over-mix.

Pour the batter into a well-buttered 9″ or 10″ spring-form pan and bake at 325° about an hour. Test after 45 minutes to see if done. Let the cake cool in the pan at least overnight. Next day, split the torte into two layers, fill with Apricot Glaze, and then spread more glaze over the top and sides. After glaze has set, ice with Chocolate Fondant.

SPANISCHE WINDTORTE *(Spanish Wind Cake)*
Photograph page 22

Schön, schöner, am schönsten: beautiful, more beautiful, most beautiful. The Viennese go one step further, *allerschönste,* the most beautiful torte of all, the super-superlative Spanish Wind Cake. (Why meringue is called Spanish Wind in Vienna is a culinary mystery.)

2 recipes Meringue Suisse (Chapter VII)
2 recipes Crème Chantilly (Chapter VIII)
2 cups sliced fresh strawberries, lightly sweetened and sprinkled with kirsch

Prepare one recipe of the meringue. Trace five 9-inch circles and one 8-inch circle on buttered and floured baking sheets. Pipe meringue in a spiral on one 9″ circle, filling the circle. (This is the base of the meringue shell.) Pipe a one-inch border of the meringue on the other four 9″ circles. Fill the 8-inch circle with a spiral of meringue and over it pipe curves and rosettes. This will be the lid of the shell. Bake all the circles as directed in the recipe for Meringue Suisse and cool.

Repeat the recipe for meringue. Place the solid 9-inch circle on a baking sheet and pipe a border of meringue around the edge. Cover with one of the 9-inch rings, pipe meringue around it and cover with another ring. Repeat until all the 9-inch rings are "cemented" together to form a shell. Ice the sides of the shell smoothly with the meringue. Pipe a border of rosettes around the base, using a medium star tube. Pipe arabesques and swags around the sides of the shell as your artistic fancy dictates. Make a "cornice" of rosettes around the top. Bake and cool the shell.

An hour before serving, prepare Crème Chantilly and fold the berries into it. Put the completed meringue shell on a serving plate, pile the Crème into it and set its cover on top. Refrigerate.

Certainly the ultimate *torte.*

ZUPPA INGLESE (*English Soup*)

Photograph page 58

This delectable Italian dessert has an origin of romance and intrigue. In 1793, Admiral Nelson met and became enamored of the beautiful Emma Lyon, Lady Hamilton, while on a diplomatic mission to Naples. He languished under her spell for several years, forgetting duties to wife and country.

During Nelson's long visit, the kingdom of Naples was in danger of being captured by Napoleon and it seemed to the king and queen—then in exile in Sicily—that only Nelson and the British fleet could save the country.

Casting aside her scruples over dealing with a woman of questionable virtue, Queen Maria Carolina prevailed upon Emma to use her influence with Lord Nelson. Emma agreed, and the result was Nelson's victory over Napoleon in the Nile in 1798, and the restoration of the king and queen to Naples.

Nelson was rewarded with a dukedom and a country palace, and Emma Lyon with a grand banquet given by the grateful people of Naples. As a fitting climax, this dessert was created by an anonymous pastry chef to honor her and the English.

"Zuppa Inglese" translates "English Soup" and it may have been invented as a counterpart of the English trifle. More likely, it was a delicious Italian joke.

> 1 recipe Génoise (**Chapter VII**)
> 1 cup rum
> 1 recipe Crème Pâtissière, flavored with almond extract (**Chapter VIII**)
> 1 recipe Crème Chantilly (**Chapter VIII**)
> **Candied violets for decoration**

Bake the Génoise in a loaf pan 4½″ x 9″. When cool, split into 3 layers. Sprinkle layers with rum. Spread Crème Pâtissière between the layers. Refrigerate for several hours. Just before serving, ice with Crème Chantilly and decorate with the candied violets.

17

SONNTAGS HASELNUSSTORTE
(Sunday Hazelnut Cake) *Photograph page 12*

Hazelnut cakes are one of the achievements of Viennese pastry-makers and this version is the most luxurious of all.

> 9 eggs
> ¾ cup sugar
> 1 cup ground hazelnuts (filberts)
> ¾ cup ground almonds
> 9 tablespoons Maraschino Liqueur
> 1 cup raspberry jam
> 1 recipe Crème Chantilly for decorating
>   (Chapter VIII)
> 1 recipe Continental Butter Cream, mocha
>   flavored (Chapter VIII)
> Whole toasted hazelnuts for garnish

Separate the eggs. Beat the yolks with the sugar until light and fluffy. Stir the ground almonds and hazelnuts together and mix with the egg yolk mixture. Beat the egg whites until stiff and gently fold them into the first mixture. Pour into 3 well-buttered 9-inch layer cake pans and bake at 350° until the cake is lightly browned and pulled away from sides of pans, about 25 minutes. Cool on racks and sprinkle each layer with 3 tablespoons of Maraschino.

Fill the layers with the raspberry jam. Ice the entire cake with the Crème Chantilly, about ¼″ or more thick. Decorate the sides of the cake with loops of the Butter Cream piped through a pastry bag, using a medium size star tube. Pipe radiating lines, like the spokes of a wheel, of the Butter Cream on the top of the cake. Pipe a 2″ circle in the center. Fill the circle with jam. Pipe rosettes of the Crème Chantilly all around the edge of the top of the cake, and around its base. Place a whole toasted hazelnut on each rosette.

I F YOU *wish to be glamorous, be a cake-baker.*

GÂTEAU LE MOKA (*Mocha Layer Cake*)

> 3 baked 7″ layers of Génoise (Chapter VII)
> 1 recipe Continental Butter Cream, mocha
> flavored (Chapter VIII)
> 1 cup chopped toasted almonds
> 1 recipe Apricot Glaze (Chapter VIII)

Reserve ½ cup of Butter Cream for decorating. Brush hot Apricot Glaze over layers, let dry a few minutes and fill with the Butter Cream. Next brush the sides of the cake with Apricot Glaze, let dry and ice top and sides with Butter Cream. Press almonds around sides of cake and decorate top all around the edge with rosettes made by forcing Butter Cream through a pastry bag fitted with a star tube.

PARIS-BREST

> ½ recipe Pâté à Chou (Chapter VII)
> ¼ cup chopped blanched almonds
> 1 egg
> 1 teaspoon cream
> 1 recipe Praline Cream (Chapter VIII)
> Confectioners' sugar for dusting

Using a large, plain pastry tube, make an 8″ circle of the Pâté à Chou on a buttered cookie sheet, about 2″ wide and ¾″ high. (Or form a circle with spoon and spatula.) Mix the egg and cream together with a fork and brush the mixture over the ring. Sprinkle with almonds. Bake at 400 degrees about 35 minutes or until golden and no beads of moisture show; then reduce heat to 350° and bake about 10 minutes longer. Cool on a rack, then cut ring in half, horizontally, and fill with Praline Cream. Replace top, put ring on serving platter and dust with a little confectioners' sugar.

To give *life to beauty, the painter uses a whole range of colours, musicians of sounds, the cook of tastes—and it is indeed remarkable that there are seven colours, seven musical notes and seven tastes.*
TENDRET

T

HE *cook is no less than an artist, and even if he may not be on the level of Polygnotus and Phidias, he has his part and his place in civilization as a whole.*
LUCIEN TENDRET

LINZERTORTE

A rich confection originating in Linz, the then-capital of upper Austria. Bake and refrigerate four or five days before you plan to serve it to give it time to mellow.

1½ cups sifted flour
¼ teaspoon salt
½ teaspoon cinnamon
½ teaspoon cloves
1 cup butter
1 cup sugar
grated rind of 1 lemon
3 egg yolks
1 cup unblanched almonds, ground
1½ cups raspberry jam
1 egg, lightly beaten
Confectioners' sugar

Sift the flour with the salt, cinnamon and cloves. Cream the butter until fluffy, add the sugar gradually and cream again. Add the grated lemon rind and mix in the egg yolks, one at a time, beating well after each addition. Then add the sifted flour mixture, alternately with the ground almonds until well blended. Wrap the dough in waxed paper and chill several hours in the refrigerator.

Roll out about ¾ of the chilled dough (keep the rest refrigerated) to about ¼″ thickness and line a 9-inch tart pan. Spread with one cup of the jam.

Roll out the remaining dough to ¼″ thickness, cut into thin strips, and make a lattice with them over the top of the torte, pressing the ends of the strips firmly against the sides. Brush with the beaten egg and bake at 350° for about 40 minutes or until golden. Cool. Fill in the spaces between the lattice with the remaining jam and dust the torte with the sifted confectioners' sugar. Store for several days before serving.

The Viennese serve thin wedges of Linzertorte with puffs of *schlag*, for in Vienna no dessert is properly presented without a whipped cream accompaniment.

Spanische Windtorte

A MAN *seldom thinks with more earnestness of anything than he does of his dinner.*
DR. JOHNSON

TARTE AUX ABRICOTS *(Apricot Tart)*
Pictured on front jacket

> ½ recipe Rich Tart Pastry (Chapter VII)
> 1 recipe Crème Pâtissière, flavored with
>   Cointreau or Curacao
> 12 or more perfect canned apricot halves
> 1 recipe Apricot Glaze (Chapter VIII)
> Cointreau or Curacao for brushing on tart shell
> ½ recipe Crème Chantilly, flavored with
>   Cointreau or Curacao

Bake the tart pastry in an 8″ tart pan or flan ring. Brush the baked tart shell with Cointreau or Curacao, and fill with Crème Pâtissière. Drain the apricots well and place them over the Crème, filling the space as closely as possible. Glaze the fruit with a hot Apricot Glaze and pipe border of Crème Chantilly around the edge of the tart. Serves 6.

Peaches may be substituted for apricots in this recipe, or you may make 8 tartlet shells, fill each with 2 tablespoons of Crème Pâtissière and finish the dessert as described above.

TARTE AUX FRAISES AU KIRSCH
(Strawberry Tart)

Follow the recipe for Tarte aux Abricots but, instead of the apricots, substitute 2 cups perfect whole strawberries, washed and dried. Flavor the Crème Pâtissière and Crème Chantilly with Kirsch instead of Cointreau or Curacao, and brush Kirsch on the baked tart shell before filling. Use Currant Glaze, instead of Apricot Glaze.

Raspberries may be substituted for strawberries, the tart then becoming Tarte aux Framboises.

VACHERIN CHANTILLY

Vacherin is the French word for a meringue "bowl" or shell. It is said that Marie Antoinette amused herself at Versailles by playing at being a cook. This is one of her decorative successes.

> 2 recipes Meringue Suisse (Chapter VII)
> 1 recipe Continental Butter Cream (Chapter VIII)
> 1 recipe Crème Chantilly (Chapter VIII)
> 2 cups fresh raspberries
> 2 tablespoons kirsch
> 2 tablespoons sugar

Trace four 8-inch circles on buttered and floured baking sheets. Fill one circle with a spiral of meringue. Pipe the other three circles with borders of the meringue about one inch wide. Make decorative rosettes with any remaining meringue. Bake as directed in Chapter VII and cool.

The shell is assembled like the one for *Spanische Windtorte* (page 16), except that the Butter Cream is the "cement" to hold the rings and base together. Use two or three tablespoons of the Butter Cream to hold each ring in place. Ice the sides and top of the *Vacherin* with the remaining Butter Cream. Set the rosettes around the top, holding them with the butter cream.

Sprinkle the berries with the Kirsch and gently fold in the sugar, being careful not to bruise the berries. Refrigerate one-half hour to blend the flavors.

An hour before serving, fold one cup of the berries into the Crème Chantilly. Pile into the *Vacherin*. Make a border of the remaining berries on top of the Crème Chantilly. Garnish with fresh mint leaves, if desired. Refrigerate until serving time.

There are many delicious variations of *Vacherin Chantilly*. Any flavor of Crème Chantilly may be used. You may fill the case with Crème Pâtissière of any flavor, instead of Crème Chantilly. Toasted slivered almonds may be pressed into the sides.

MILLE FEUILLES (*Napoleon Cake*)

The creation of the original "Thousand Leaves" cake is attributed to Carême. Its more familiar name, "Napoleon," does not refer to the Little Corporal, but is a corruption of *Napolitain,* a reference to the Neapolitan custom of making desserts in contrasting layers.

½ recipe Puff Paste (Chapter VII)
1 recipe Crème Plombières (Chapter VIII)
1 cup Wilton Fondant (Chapter VIII)
⅓ cup Chocolate Fondant (Chapter VIII)

Roll out the Puff Paste to a 16-inch square, ⅛" thick. Trim with a sharp knife into three strips 5" x 15". Place strips on a cookie sheet, prick all over with a fork and put in freezer for one hour. Bake at 350° for about 35 minutes, or until puffed and golden.

Fill the layers with the Crème Plombières and ice the top with Fondant.

Fit a small pastry bag with a plain small tube and fill it with the Chocolate Fondant. Working quickly, pipe fine lines one inch apart, horizontally across the top of the cake. Draw the blade of a table knife the length of the cake through the chocolate lines in opposing directions to give the cake its characteristic "marbled" look.

GÂTEAU ROLLA

1 recipe Swiss Broyage (Chapter VII)
1 recipe Continental Butter Cream, mocha flavored (Chapter VIII)
1 cup blanched slivered toasted almonds
Sifted confectioners' sugar

Bake the broyage in five 6-inch circles. Sandwich them with butter cream, spread thinly. Do not ice top layer. Ice the sides of the cake with the remaining Butter Cream and press the almonds into them. Put a 6-inch lace paper doily on top and sift the confectioners' sugar thinly over it. Carefully remove doily and the sugar will have left a lacy design. Refrigerate 24 hours.

IN *excess, nectar poisons*
EASTERN PROVERB

S OME *people have a foolish way of not minding, or of pretending not to mind, what they eat. For my part I mind my belly very studiously and carefully for I look upon it that he who does not mind his belly will hardly mind anything else.*
DR. JOHNSON

DOBOS TORTA

One of the most spectacular creations of Budapest—a traditional holiday treat.

> 1 recipe Génoise (Chapter VII)
> 2 recipes Uncooked Chocolate Butter Icing (Chapter VIII)
> ⅔ cup sugar
> 1 cup coarsely chopped almonds or hazelnuts (optional)

Butter well, and dust with flour, the bottoms of three 8″ spring-form pans. (Or use 8″ layer cake pans, buttered, lined with waxed paper, then buttered again and dusted with flour.) Spread 3 or 4 tablespoons (or to a depth of no more than ¼″) of Génoise batter in each and bake in a 400° oven for about 8 minutes, or until lightly browned. Carefully remove from pan and peel off paper. Place cakes on rack to cool. Repeat until all batter is used, and you have 8 to 12 layers.

Place a layer on a serving plate, spread with icing and cover with a second layer. Repeat until all layers are used. Do not ice top layer. (Reserve about 1 cup of icing for sides of cake.)

Melt the sugar without stirring in a skillet until it carmelizes. Spread this quickly on top of cake with a hot knife. Mark the cake into serving portions with radiating lines like spokes of a wheel using the hot knife. Ice the sides of the cake with the chocolate icing and, if you wish, press the nuts into the iced sides. Chill 12 to 24 hours before serving.

Gâteaux de Grandes Fêtes

BÛCHE DE NOËL (*French Yule Log Cake*)

A traditional cake served all over France at Christmas.

> 1 recipe Basic Sponge Sheet (Chapter VII)
> ½ cup sifted confectioners' sugar
>   (or as needed)
> 1 recipe Continental Butter Cream, mocha
>   flavored (Chapter VIII)
> 1 recipe Crème Chantilly (Chapter VIII)

Bake the Sponge Sheet in a jelly roll pan about 11" x 16". Sprinkle a tea towel with confectioners' sugar. As soon as the Sponge Sheet has baked, take it out of the oven and invert on the towel, so the waxed paper is on top. Do not remove wax paper. Roll the cake tightly in the towel to a 16-inch long cylinder. Cool, carefully unroll and peel off the wax paper. Trim off the crusty edges and spread the cake thinly with Butter Cream, then thickly with Crème Chantilly. Reserve the rest of the Butter Cream. Reroll and refrigerate for half an hour.

Cut a small piece off each end of the cake, diagonally, and place on either side of the "log" with the diagonals against the cake.

Put the rest of the Butter Cream into a pastry bag fitted with a star tube and pipe long lines of the Butter Cream over the entire "log" to resemble bark. Pipe the Butter Cream in a spiral over the cut ends. Refrigerate until serving time.

Bûche de Noël is sometimes made with Chocolate Sponge Sheet.

H ALLO! *A great deal
of steam! the
pudding was out of
the copper. A smell
like a washing day!
That was the cloth.
A smell like an eating-
house and a pastry-
cook's next door to
each other, with a
laundress's next
door to that! That
was the pudding!
In half a minute
Mrs. Cratchit
entered—flushed
but smiling proudly—
with the pudding,
like a speckled
cannon ball, so hard
and firm, blazing in
half of a half-a-
quartern of ignited
brandy, and bedight
with Christmas holly
stuck into the top."*

ENGLISH PLUM PUDDING

All the gaiety, good eating and good cheer that went on at Bob Cratchit's house is symbolized in Plum Pudding—so firmly entrenched in England's Christmas traditions that it is often called a Christmas Pudding.

¾ cup dried currants
1 cup seedless raisins
1 cup white raisins
⅜ cup finely chopped candied fruit peel
 (mixed fruits)
⅜ cup candied cherries, finely chopped
½ cup blanched slivered almonds
1 small tart apple, cored and coarsely
 chopped
½ carrot, scraped and coarsely chopped
1 tablespoon finely grated orange peel
1 teaspoon finely grated lemon peel
¼ pound beef suet, finely chopped
1 cup flour
2 cups fine crumbs of fresh white bread
½ cup dark brown sugar
½ teaspoon ground allspice
½ teaspoon salt
3 eggs
½ cup brandy
¼ cup fresh orange juice
2 tablespoons fresh lemon juice
¼ cup brandy for flaming

Place the first eleven ingredients in a large bowl and stir them with your hands till well mixed. Sift the flour with the allspice and salt and add to the fruit mixture. Mix well. Then add the bread crumbs and brown sugar and mix again.

In a separate bowl, beat the eggs until fluffy, add the one-half cup of brandy and the orange and lemon juice. Stir well. Pour this mixture over the fruit mixture and knead together with your hands until well blended. Cover with a damp towel and refrigerate at least 12 hours.

Butter two 1-quart pudding molds, spoon in the pudding, adjust the covers tightly and butter the seams where the covers meet the sides of the molds. (The English use a bowl-shaped mold without a cover and tie a floured cloth over the rim with a string.)

Put the molds on trivets placed in a large kettle and pour in boiling water. The water should come three quarters of the way up the sides of the molds. Bring to a boil, cover the kettle, reduce the heat and simmer for eight hours. Add more boiling water as needed to keep the level constant.

When the puddings are done, take them out of the water, remove the covers and cool to room temperature. Replace the covers (or cover with foil) and refrigerate at least 3 weeks. (Plum puddings used to be made a year in advance and kept in a cool place for the following Christmas!)

To serve, place the molds on trivets in the kettle, pour in boiling water as before, cover the kettle, bring to a boil and simmer for 2 hours. Loosen the sides with a knife and invert pudding on a serving plate. Stick a sprig of holly in the center of each pudding, warm the brandy, ignite and pour over the pudding.

Serve with chilled Brandy Hard Sauce or Hot Rum Sauce (Chapter VIII).

29

SFINGI SAN GIUSEPPE *(St. Joseph's Puffs)*

This is one of the delicacies served at "St. Joseph's table" on March 19 in Italy. On this day, each citizen contributes flowers, food or cash to an outdoor banquet. Waifs, widows and beggars are invited to eat their fill along with the assembled townspeople. Many Italian communities in the United States still continue the colorful custom.

> 1 recipe Pâté à Chou (Chapter VII)
> 1 tablespoon sugar
> 1 teaspoon grated lemon rind
> 1 teaspoon grated orange rind
> 1 teaspoon vanilla

When making the Pâté à Chou, add the sugar to the water, butter and salt while heating. Add the orange and lemon rinds to the paste after the eggs have been beaten in. Bake as directed for Pâté à Chou and fill with the following mixture:

> 2 cups well-drained ricotta cheese
> 3 tablespoons sugar
> 5 ounces chopped semi-sweet chocolate
> 3 tablespoons rum or liqueur
> Confectioners' sugar for dusting

Put the drained ricotta through a strainer and beat until very smooth. Fold in the remaining ingredients. Fill the puffs and dust with sifted confectioners' sugar.

CROQUEMBOUCHE *(Cream Puff Tower)*

Photograph page 40

An impressive *Pièce Montée* that should be attempted only in dry weather. The name translates "crumble in the mouth" (the effect of the hardened caramel). This recipe is from an 1870 cookbook.

> ⅓ **recipe Puff Paste (Chapter VII)**
> 1 **recipe Pâté à Chou (Chapter VII)**
> 1 **recipe Crème Pâtissière, any flavor**
> **(Chapter VIII)**
> 2 **recipes Caramel Syrup (Chapter VIII)**

Roll out puff paste to a ¼″ thick 9″ circle. Chill, prick all over with a fork and bake. Place on a serving platter.

Bake 36 or more little cream puffs with the Pâté and fill them with the Crème.

Make one recipe of the Caramel Syrup. Dip the puffs, one at a time, into the syrup and arrange them around the edge of the puff paste circle, using about 12 puffs.

Continue dipping and piling the puffs one on another in narrowing circles, pyramid fashion. Make the second recipe of Caramel Syrup when the first has been used. Use one puff to crown the top. Pour over any remaining syrup. (Be careful in using the hot syrup. Sugar burns are very painful!)

Garnish with curved shapes of baked Pâté à Chou (as in our picture) or with candied cherries and frills of whipped cream. To serve, detach puffs from the tower with a serving fork and spoon, beginning at the top.

LISA'S APPLECAKE

The recipe for this cake (really a tart) has been in wine consultant Sig Langstadter's family for generations. Here it is, just as it was translated from the German. "So good you can't believe it".

　¼ **pound stick plus 1 tablespoon butter**
　1 **egg**
　1 **egg yolk**
　⅓ ⎫
　¼ ⎬ **cup sugar**
　⅓ ⎭
　1 **teaspoon baking powder**
　2 **cups plus 2 level tablespoons sifted flour**
　½ **egg shell** *cold* **water**
　cinnamon
　3 **pounds tart apples**
　(**all ingredients should be cold**)

Mix the baking powder and flour and sift into a large bowl. Make a well in the center and add the butter, ⅓ cup of sugar, the egg and ½ eggshell of cold water. With your hands mix everything as quickly as possible and knead until it is of smooth consistency. Wrap in wax paper and chill.

Now peel the apples, cut in quarters, core and slice them thin. Butter a 9 or 10-inch springform pan. Take the dough from the refrigerator, break off about ⅓ and put it back in the refrigerator. Press the remaining ⅔ into the pan with your hands, covering the bottom and about ¾ up the sides. Put in apples and sprinkle with the ¼ cup of sugar. Take the rest of the dough from the refrigerator and roll it out on a lightly-floured board. (Roll to about an 11″ circle to provide a surface large enough to cover the apples). To avoid tearing this thin cake-cover, first loosen it from the board very carefully with a spatula, dust the dough ever so lightly with flour, put the rolling pin down on it very gently, carefully roll the dough around the pin, then cover the apples with it.

Seal the dough around the edge by crimping or pressing it down.

Mix the egg yolk with a few drops of *cold* water and brush the top with it. Sprinkle on a little cinnamon and the rest of the sugar (⅛ cup). Bake in a preheated 375° oven for about 1 hour, or until crisp and golden brown. Serve slightly warm or cold. It is delicious either way, plain or topped with whipped cream.

TARTE AUX POMMES (*Apple Tart*)

> 1 recipe Rich Tart Pastry (Chapter VII), chilled
> 3 pounds tart apples
> 1 lemon, grated rind and juice
> ½ cup water
> ½ cup raisins
> ½ to 1 cup sugar
> 1 tablespoon milk
> 2 tablespoons cinnamon sugar (add a few shakes of cinnamon to the sugar)
> Apricot Glaze (Chapter VIII)

Peel, core and cut apples into thick slices. Place in a heavy saucepan with lemon juice and rind and about ½ cup of water. Cover and cook over low heat about 10 minutes. When apples begin to steam, remove cover, stir and cook a few more minutes until just tender. Add raisins and sugar to taste. Cool.

Roll the chilled tart pastry to ⅛" thickness and fit it into a 9" flan ring or 9" tart mold. Chill well or freeze. Roll trimmings from tart shell ⅛" thick. Cut in strips ½" wide and 10" in length. Sprinkle with cinnamon sugar.

Fill chilled tart shell with apple slices, placed in a radiating design, and make a lattice of the pastry strips on top. Bake on lowest shelf of 350° oven about 1 hour. Raise to higher shelf to brown for 15 minutes more. Cool, then brush with Apricot Glaze.

GÂTEAU SAINT-HONORÉ

One of the most beautiful French cakes, named after Honoré, the Bishop of Amiens about 660. He is the patron saint of pastry chefs.

FILLING:

> 2 recipes Crème Pâtissière (Chapter VIII)
> 1½ ounces gelatin
> ⅓ cup cold water
> 6 egg whites
> ⅛ teaspoon salt
> 2 tablespoons confectioners' sugar

Prepare Créme Pâtissiére, reserve ¾ cup and chill. Soften gelatin in water for a few minutes, then add to the remaining hot Crème, and stir till blended and cool. Whip the egg whites till stiff with the salt and confectioners' sugar. Fold into the cooled Crème Pâtissière. Refrigerate.

SHELL

> 1 recipe Pâté à Chou (Chapter VII)
> ⅓ recipe Puff Paste (Chapter VII)

Roll out the puff paste, trim to a 9 ″ circle, and put on a buttered cookie sheet. Chill well and prick all over. Brush edge with cold water.

Using a pastry bag and large plain tube, pipe a ring of pâté à chou around the edge of the puff paste in an even roll about 1″ thick. Bake as for cream puffs. Make walnut-size puffs of the remaining pâté and bake.

CARAMEL SYRUP:

> (See Chapter VIII)

ASSEMBLY:

Fill the tiny puffs with the reserved ¾ cup of Crème Pâtissière. Dip the base of each of the puffs in syrup (holding with a tong) and place on top of the prepared shell to make a high wall. Pile the filling in the center. Garnish each puff with half a candied cherry, and decorate the cake with frills of whipped cream.

TELL ME *what you eat and I will tell you what you are.*
BRILLAT-SAVARIN

E MAY *live
without books—
what is knowledge
but grieving?
He may live
without hope—
what is hope
but deceiving?
He may live
without love—
what is passion
but pining?
But where is the man
who can live
without dining?*
OWEN MEREDITH

PITHIVIERS

The main claim to fame of the French town of Pithiviers, where it was created hundreds of years ago.

½ recipe Puff Paste (Chapter VII)
½ recipe Frangipane Cream (Chapter VIII)
1 egg yolk
1 teaspoon cream
Confectioners' sugar for sprinkling

Roll the chilled Puff Paste to ¼″ thickness. Cut into two 8″ circles, using a scalloped cutter. Place one circle on an unbuttered baking sheet. Spread with the Frangipane Cream to within ½ inch of edge. Moisten edge with cold water. Score the other circle with a sharp knife into a pattern of arcs radiating from the center. Place over first circle and press edges together. Chill well.

Mix the egg yolks with the cream and brush the top of the cake. Dust liberally with the sugar and bake in a 350° oven until cake is golden, about 1 hour.

SCHWARZWÄLDER KIRSCHTORTE
(*Black Forest Cherry Cake*)

1 recipe Chocolate Sponge Sheet
   (Chapter VII)
⅓ cup Kirsch
1 recipe Continental Butter Cream, chocolate
   flavored (Chapter VIII)
2 cups pitted black sweet cherries, cut
   in half (fresh or canned)
1 recipe Crème Chantilly, flavored with
   Kirsch (Chapter VIII)
Chocolate Curls (next page)

Bake the sponge sheet in two 9″ layers. Cool slightly and sprinkle each layer with the Kirsch. Cool completely. Spread one layer with Chocolate Butter Cream, and press 1½ cups of the cherries into the cream. Top with the second layer. Spread Crème Chantilly on top and sides of the cake. Decorate with swirls of the Crème, chocolate curls and the remaining cherries.

35

CHOCOLATE CURLS

Melt 3 ounces of semi-sweet chocolate, stir until smooth and pour onto a flat platter or marble slab. Spread to a 6″ circle. Cool until firm. Draw the sharp edge of the blade of a paring knife across the chocolate, holding the knife parallel to platter, to peel off the chocolate in curls.

ENGLISH TRIFLE

Not a trifling dessert, but a magnificent concoction of cake, custard, fruit and cream, liberally laced with spirits! A dessert to be taken very seriously. There are many variations of trifle—this is one of the most lavish.

> 1 recipe Génoise (Chapter VII)
> 1 cup strawberry jam
> 1 cup Cream Sherry
> ¼ cup brandy
> 1 recipe Custard Sauce, chilled (Chapter VIII)
> 1 recipe Crème Chantilly, flavored with rum (Chapter VIII)
> 1 pint fresh strawberries, cleaned and cut in halves
> Toasted almonds for garnish

Bake the Génoise in an 8″ springform pan. Cool and split into two layers. Place one layer in a glass serving dish, about 9″ in diameter. Sprinkle with half of the sherry. Spread with the jam. Top with the second layer of cake. Mix the brandy with the remaining sherry and sprinkle over the cake. Let stand until all the liquid has been absorbed.

Pour the custard sauce over the cake and refrigerate an hour or more. At serving time, spread with half of the Crème Chantilly, and arrange the berries in a decorative design in the center. Fill a pastry bag with the remaining Crème Chantilly and pipe decorative swirls all around the edge. Garnish with toasted almonds.

CHAPTER II

THREE STAR DESSERTS

From Angelica to Zabaglione "three star" as applied to these desserts means just one thing: Superlative!

Though less heroic than the splendid pastries in the first chapter, these desserts have just as impressive a lineage. Many were created by the great chefs of Europe and—like such pastries as Spanische Windtorte and Gâteau Saint-Honoré—all of these are equally a part of the precious heritage from the golden age of cuisine.

Soufflés, parfaits, mousses . . . ravishing fruit desserts . . . dramatic chafing dish productions—they are all here, because of one common quality. They are superlative, "three star."

CHOOSE *eggs oblong,*
Remember they'll be
found
Of sweeter taste and
whiter than the
round.
HORACE

LEMON SOUFFLÉ

The cook who has mastered the simple art of creating worthy soufflés can count on applause every performance. Louis Eustache Ude makes this comment about the famous dessert form in *The French Cook* (1813): "If sent up in time, they are very good eating; if not, they are no better than other puddings".

> ⅓ cup sugar
> 3 tablespoons flour
> ¾ cup milk
> 4 egg yolks, lightly beaten
> 2 tablespoons butter
> ¼ cup Galliano liqueur
> 2 teaspoons grated lemon peel
> 2 tablespoons lemon juice
> 5 egg whites
> ⅛ teaspoon salt

Butter bottom and sides of a 1-quart soufflé dish. Make a collar for the dish by cutting a double strip of foil four inches wide. Butter it and secure it around the top of the dish with string. Sprinkle both dish and collar with sugar.

Blend the ⅓ cup sugar and flour in saucepan. Stir in milk gradually. Cook, stirring constantly, until sauce boils 1 minute. Stir small amount of sauce into egg yolks and return this to saucepan. Add butter. Continue to cook, stirring constantly, till sauce thickens. Blend sauce with Galliano, lemon peel and juice in a large bowl. Beat egg whites with salt till stiff and fold into egg yolk mixture. Pour into prepared dish and bake 35 to 40 minutes at 375°, or until knife inserted in center comes out clean. Serve immediately, plain, with whipped cream or with lemon sauce (Chapter VIII).

To make a "crown" on the soufflé, make a groove with a knife about 1½" from the edge of the dish all around the top before baking.

Croquembouche

CHOCOLATE SOUFFLÉ

Follow the recipe for Lemon Soufflé (page 38) but omit the lemon juice, grated lemon rind and Galliano. Add 3 ounces of **melted unsweetened chocolate** to the thickened hot sauce before stirring in the egg yolks. When the sauce has been removed from the heat, stir in **one-fourth cup brandy** or **Crème de Cacao** before folding in egg whites.

Serve immediately with Chocolate Fudge Sauce or Chocolate Bittersweet Sauce (Chapter VIII).

SALZBURGER NOCKERLN

The airiest of the innumerable *mehlspeisen* that the Austrian cook has at her fingertips. The texture is much like that of a soufflé.

ALL *griefs with bread are less*
ENGLISH PROVERB

>   4 egg yolks
>   ¼ cup flour
>   8 egg whites
>   ¾ cup sugar
>   1 tablespoon vanilla
>   3 tablespoons butter
>   Confectioners' sugar for dusting

Beat the egg yolks till light and fluffy, gradually beat in the flour. Beat the egg whites until very stiff, add the sugar a little at a time. Add vanilla. Melt the butter in an 8″ skillet, tilting to coat the sides. Heat till it bubbles. Quickly fold the egg white and egg yolk mixtures together, and spoon into the skillet in 6 puffs. Sauté only a minute or two, until the undersides are lightly colored. Put the pan in a 250° oven and bake about 10 minutes until the top is golden. Dust liberally with confectioners' sugar and serve at once.

THE DISCOVERY *of a new dish does more for the happiness of the human race than the discovery of a new star.*
BRILLAT-SAVARIN

FRUITS RAFRAÎCHIS AU KIRSCH
(Fresh Fruit Compote)

Simplest and most beautiful of all desserts, fresh fruit, is often the ideal ending to an elaborate meal. The cook may free her imagination in combining the fruits, choosing whatever is in season and pleases the eye and palate. Balls of various melons—honeydew, watermelon, cantaloupe—with diced fresh pineapple is one delicious combination. Sliced fresh peaches, bananas and halved strawberries another. Orange wedges, bananas, sweet black cherries and pineapple is a third choice.

Clean and prepare the fruits and arrange them attractively in a silver or crystal bowl. Sprinkle with sugar and pour over them one or two ounces of kirsch. Chill for several hours to blend the flavors. Before bringing to the table, you may embed the bowl in a large bowl filled with crushed ice.

There is also a wide latitude on the choice of liqueurs used to marinate the fruits. Rum, peach brandy, curacao, galliano or cointreau can be used according to your taste.

Fruits Rafraîchis au Normandie consists of slices of tart apples, fresh pineapple and banana, sweetened and soaked in Calvados. It is served with whipped cream, Calvados-flavored.

Fruits Rafraîchis Tzarine (fresh fruit Czarina) combines mixed fruits and kummel and is served on a bed of pineapple ice cream, and covered with Crème Chantilly decorated with candied violets and angelica.

PÊCHES MELBA

Auguste Escoffier, titled "the emperor of the world's kitchens", gives this account of his most famous dessert: "Madame Nellie Melba, the *grande cantrice* of Australia, sang at Covent Garden in 1894. She stayed at the Savoy Hotel . . . at which time I was directing the kitchens of that establishment. One evening when *Lohengrin* was to be performed, Madam Melba gave me two seats. As you know, in that opera, a swan appears. The following evening Madame Melba gave a *petite souper* for several friends . . . and to show her that I had profited agreeably from the seats she had graciously offered me, I sculpted from a block of ice a superb swan, and between the two wings I buried a silver bowl. I covered the bottom of the bowl with vanilla ice cream and on this bed of ice cream I placed peaches soaked in a syrup of vanilla. A puree of fresh raspberries covered the peaches completely. Thus deliciously completed, this dessert was to become world famous . . ."

Here, without the sculpted swan, is Escoffier's recipe.

> **3 ripe peaches**
> **1 cup sugar**
> **1 cup water**
> **1-inch piece of vanilla bean**
> **6 scoops vanilla ice cream**
> **Sauce Melba (Chapter VIII)**

Plunge the peaches into boiling water, slip off their skins, cut them in half and remove the pits. Boil the water and sugar with the vanilla bean for 5 minutes. Poach the peaches in the syrup for a few minutes until barely tender. Chill the fruit. Put the ice cream in a silver or crystal bowl, lay the peaches (rounded side up) on the ice cream, and pour over all the raspberry Sauce Melba.

Later M. Escoffier further embellished his creation by adding a sprinkling of toasted almonds.

L**UCENT** *syrups...*
spiced dainties,
every one. From
silken Samarkand to
cedared Lebanon.
KEATS

GREEK ORANGES

Here is a ravishingly beautiful dessert with an equally ravishing flavor. It takes some trouble and time, but your guests' approval of your efforts should be a fitting reward.

> **6 whole oranges**
> **4 cups sugar**
> **2 cups water**
> **few drops of red food coloring**

Pare off the colored skin of 4 of the oranges, being careful not to take any of the white membrane. (A potato peeler will speed this task). Julienne this peel into tiny slivers.

Place the orange peel in a small saucepan of boiling water, continue boiling for ten minutes and drain. Repeat this twice more—total of three boilings and three drainings.

Trim off the skin and white membrane of all the oranges and discard. Put the oranges in a heat-proof bowl.

Stir the sugar and water together and boil for 10 minutes. Pour the hot syrup over the oranges and let stand for fifteen minutes. Then drain off the syrup, add the red food coloring and boil it again for 15 minutes.

Sprinkle the oranges with the julienne of orange peel, and again pour the hot syrup over them. Cool to room temperature and serve in a footed glass bowl. These are best if not refrigerated.

CHERRIES IN RED WINE

One of the jewels of Swiss cuisine is magnificent fruit, which is served in many imaginative ways. This is a superb cherry dessert from the Italian-speaking province of Ticino where the orchards are especially fine.

2 cups of fresh sweet cherries
sugar
grated rind of 1 lemon
1 cup of good dry red wine

Stone the cherries and put them in a small saucepan. Sprinkle with sugar, the amount depending on the sweetness of the fruit. Next sprinkle on lemon rind and allow to stand at room temperature for 30 minutes to an hour. Pour wine over cherries, adding more, if necessary to cover. Bring to a boil and remove from heat. Chill.

PEACHES IN WINE

This delightful fruit originated in Persia, hence its old name, *persica*. Peaches flourished in the region around Paris and Louis XIV took a special interest in their cultivation. They did less well in England, and were considered so fragile that, when ripe, they were immediately treated to a wine preservative. This, understandably, heightened their flavor. This recipe is from an eighteenth century English cookbook.

6 large fresh peaches
1½ cups Rhine wine
1 cup sugar
1 teaspoon cinnamon
Rind of 1 lemon
¼ cup Clarified Butter (Chapter VII)

Peel the peaches, cut them in halves, reserve the stones. Slice the lemon rind thinly. Mix the wine, sugar, cinnamon and lemon rind. Pour this mixture over the peaches and marinate them for several hours, turning them often. Wrap the peach stones in a cloth, pound with a hammer to break, and remove the kernels. Split and reserve. Dry the peaches and sauté gently in the butter. Heat the marinade without stirring until it carmelizes, turning thick and golden. Arrange the peaches in a serving dish. Scatter the kernels over them, pour over the caramelized wine, and serve hot.

A BIT *in the morning*
is better than
nothing all day
ENGLISH PROVERB

POIRES HÉLÈNE *(Pears Hélène)*

A delicious dessert that combines the complimentary flavors of chocolate and fresh pears.

> 1¼ cups of sugar
> 2 cups of water
> 1-inch piece of vanilla bean
> 6 ripe pears
> 1 quart vanilla ice cream
> 1 recipe Chocolate Fudge Sauce (Chapter VIII)

Blend together sugar, water and vanilla bean and bring mixture to a boil for 5 minutes. Peel the pears and poach them in the syrup until they are tender, or until they become somewhat transparent and are easily pierced by a wooden skewer. Allow pears to cool in the syrup before draining. Chill.

Serve pears on vanilla ice cream and cover with Hot Chocolate Sauce.

STRAWBERRIES ROMANOFF

As early as 1560, mention was made of the popularity of strawberries and cream as an evening dessert. This was a particular favorite of the ladies of Henri II's court. Here is the deluxe Russian version of this classic. Rum or Kirsch may replace the Cointreau.

> 1 pint vanilla ice cream
> 1 cup heavy cream, whipped
> juice of 1 lemon
> 6 tablespoons Cointreau
> 2 quarts strawberries, lightly sugared
> Whole berries for garnish

Clean, hull and cut the berries in half. Sprinkle with a little sugar and chill for an hour or more. Soften the ice cream slightly and fold in the whipped cream, lemon juice and Cointreau. Pour the cream mixture over the berries and blend gently. Serve in chilled dessert dishes. Garnish with whole berries.

HOT FRUIT COMPOTE

This is the winter version of *Fruits Rafraîchis* and is equally delicious and attractive. The fruits achieve a mellow, somewhat caramel flavor as they heat.

Choose a compatible group from the large variety of excellent canned fruits. Apricots, pears and pineapple wedges—Mandarin orange segments, thickly-sliced fresh banana and peach halves are two possibilities.

Drain the fruits, arrange them in an oven-proof dish and sprinkle over them broken walnut meats or shaved pecans, if desired. Or add a few maraschino cherries for color. Mix the reserved fruit juices with an equal quantity of medium-dry sherry—about a cup of liquid in all. Pour over the fruits. (There should be enough to nearly cover them.)

Bake uncovered at 300° for an hour. Serve hot.

FRESH FRUIT FOOL

In England the word *fool* was synonymous with *trifle*, so cooks of the past considered this a trifling dessert. It is really a delicate, delicious summer treat.

> 1 quart fresh gooseberries, raspberries, blackberries or strawberries
> 1 cup sugar (approximate)
> 3 cups heavy cream

Place the fruit in a heavy saucepan and simmer for half an hour, stirring with a large wooden spoon to extract the juice. Stir in the sugar, mix well and continue to simmer until the sugar is dissolved. Taste and add more sugar, if needed. Remove from heat and force through a fine sieve. Cool and refrigerate.

Beat the cream until stiff and gently fold the fruit purée into it. Do not overmix—there should be mingled streaks of fruit and cream. Serve at once in parfait glasses.

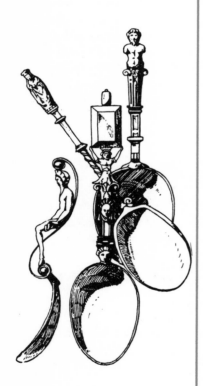

BAVARIAN CREAM

Spectacular in taste and appearance, this most deluxe pudding was the rage of the continent in the Victorian era. It's just as luxurious today.

> 1 ounce gelatin
> ¼ cup cold water
> 1 cup milk
> 1 inch piece vanilla bean
> ⅜ cup sugar
> 4 egg yolks
> pinch of salt
> 1 cup heavy cream, stiffly whipped
> Additional whipped cream and fruit for garnish

Soak the gelatin in cold water. Mix the milk with the sugar in the top of a double boiler, add the vanilla bean and scald. Beat the egg yolks and salt in a large bowl until thick and lemon-colored.

Pour a little of the hot milk into the beaten yolks, stir quickly and pour gradually into the hot milk mixture, stirring constantly. Cook over 1″ of simmering water about 10 minutes, stirring constantly, or until the mixture coats the spoon.

Pour into a large bowl, discard vanilla bean, add gelatin and stir until gelatin is dissolved and mixture is cool. Chill until custard starts to thicken. Gently fold in cream. Pour into a one-quart mold. Chill several hours or overnight.

Unmold on serving platter and garnish with fresh berries or slices of fruit and frills of whipped cream forced through a pastry tube. Serves 6.

CHOCOLATE BAVARIAN CREAM

Melt 2 ounces unsweetened chocolate and stir into scalded milk-sugar mixture. Replace the vanilla bean with 1 tablespoon rum or brandy, stirred into the cooling custard.

POLITICAL *issues are decided at the table. Talleyrand has often been indebted for his successes to the skilful creations of Antonin Carême.*
TENDRET

CHARLOTTE RUSSE

Here is the recipe created by the master-chef Carême to please Czar Alexander I.

30 or more lady fingers
1 recipe Bavarian cream

Line a straight-sided Charlotte mold with the lady fingers, cutting them in diamond shapes to line the bottom of the mold in the shape of a flower, and upright all around the sides. Fill the mold with the Bavarian cream. Chill several hours, or overnight, and unmold on a silver platter. Garnish as you like with fresh berries or candied fruits and frills of whipped cream.

It is easier to unmold the Charlotte if you line the mold with wax paper before adding lady fingers.

CHOCOLATE SUPRÊME
Picture on back of book jacket

This is truly a 3-star dessert, simple to prepare but lavish in its flavor and effect.

1 cup semisweet chocolate morsels
4 eggs, separated
1 teaspoon of hot water
4 or 5 drops of vanilla
1 tablespoon brandy
1 cup heavy cream, whipped
Shaved, unsweetened chocolate for garnish

Melt the chocolate, cool and beat in egg yolks, one at a time. Add hot water, vanilla and brandy. Fold into this mixture the egg whites, beaten stiff. Spoon into small glass punch cups.

Chill several hours (preferably over night) and serve with whipped cream, garnished with shaved chocolate. Serves four.

CHOCOLATE MOUSSE

    1 ounce gelatin
    1 cup milk
    ½ cup sugar, divided
    ⅛ teaspoon salt
    2 eggs, separated
    6 ounces (1 cup) semi-sweet chocolate morsels
    ½ teaspoon vanilla
    1 cup heavy cream, whipped
    ½ recipe Crème Chantilly for Decorating
        (Chapter VIII)
    Chocolate Curls (page 36)

Sprinkle gelatin over milk in small saucepan. Add ¼ cup of sugar, salt, egg yolks and chocolate morsels and stir until thoroughly mixed. Place over low heat, stirring constantly, until gelatin is completely dissolved and chocolate is melted. Remove from heat and beat until chocolate is blended. Stir in vanilla and chill, stirring occasionally, until the mixture mounds slightly when it is dropped from a spoon.

Beat egg whites until stiff and gradually add remaining ¼ cup of sugar. Beat until very stiff and then fold into chocolate mixture. Next fold in whipped cream. Turn into an oiled mold and refrigerate several hours until firm. Turn out on a serving plate and garnish with swirls and rosettes of the Crème Chantilly. Sprinkle with Chocolate Curls.

RASPBERRY MOUSSE

    ½ cup sugar
    1 cup water
    2 cups washed raspberries
    1 ounce gelatin
    ⅓ cup cold water
    3 egg whites
    1 cup heavy cream
    ½ recipe Crème Chantilly for Decorating
        (Chapter VIII)
    1 cup raspberries for garnish

Combine the sugar and 1 cup water in a saucepan and boil until it becomes a thin syrup. Add the berries and cook gently until just soft. Press through a sieve.

Soften the gelatin in the ⅛ cup cold water and add it to the hot purée. Stir to dissolve thoroughly. Then cool.

Beat 3 egg whites till stiff and fold into the purée. Lightly whip the cream till just thickened. Add to the purée mixture, place the bowl in a pan of cracked ice and beat until the mixture is quite thick. Turn into an oiled mold and chill in the refrigerator several hours. Turn out on a serving plate, decorate with Crème Chantilly forced through a pastry tube, and surround with chilled fresh raspberries.

SOUFFLÉ DE NOËL

This is not actually a soufflé, but a refreshing lemon-flavored mousse. It is delicious any time of the year.

> **6 egg yolks**
> **¼ cup sugar**
> **juice of 3 lemons**
> **grated rind of 2 lemons**
> **1 ounce gelatin**
> **2 tablespoons cold water**
> **1 cup heavy cream, whipped till stiff with a dash**
> **of salt and a dash of powdered ginger**

Put the egg yolks and sugar in a sauce pan over the lowest flame, and beat with a whisk till light and creamy. Do not let the mixture boil. Remove from the fire and stir in the lemon juice and rind, and allow the mixture to cool.

Soak the gelatin in the cold water for 5 minutes, set over a very low flame and stir till dissolved. Strain it through a fine sieve into the cold egg yolk mixture.

Fold in the whipped cream mixture, pour into a silver or crystal bowl and chill until set.

Garnish with whipped cream, candied fruits and citron.

PARFAIT AU GRAND MARNIER

> 7 egg yolks
> 1 cup sugar syrup
> 3 tablespoons Grand Marnier
> grated rind of 1 orange
> juice of 1 orange
> 1 cup heavy cream, whipped
> ½ recipe Crème Chantilly for Decorating,
>   flavored with Grand Marnier (Chapter VIII)
> Slivers of candied orange peel

Make the sugar syrup by combining 3 ounces of water (slightly less than half a cup) and 1¼ cups of sugar in a heavy saucepan. Cook over a low heat for 5 minutes. Cool the syrup before adding it to the parfait.

Put the egg yolks in a heavy saucepan and beat till they are light and fluffy. Then place the saucepan over low heat and gradually add the sugar syrup, beating all the time. Continue beating till the mixture is thick and smooth. Remove from heat and beat until cool. Then add the orange rind, juice and Grand Marnier, mixing well. Fold in the whipped cream. Pour into a fancy mold, rinsed in cold water, and cover it with its own cover. (If mold does not have a cover, make one with doubled aluminum foil.) Freeze until solid.

Unmold on a silver platter, decorate with the Crème Chantilly piped through a pastry tube. Finish the decoration with slivers of candied orange peel.

This recipe will serve six generously. Double it for a big dinner party.

BISCUIT TORTONI

Biscuit tortoni is an Italian version of a parfait, very simple to make and serve, and enthusiastically received by all ages.

½ cup macaroon crumbs (dry macaroons in a
  slow oven and crush finely with a rolling pin)
1 cup heavy cream
3 tablespoons confectioners' sugar
1 tablespoon rum
1 egg white, beaten stiff
chopped toasted almonds for garnish

Whip the cream until thick but not stiff. Fold in sugar
and rum. Beat till stiff and blend in the macaroon crumbs.
Fold in the egg white, spoon the mixture into fluted paper
cups, and sprinkle the tops with almonds. Put the cups
in a refrigerator tray and freeze until firm.

ANGELICA

An old-fashioned, heavenly parfait that lives up to its
name. When the table is cleared after a robustly-
flavored entree, carry in this dessert in all its pristine
whiteness on a silver tray.

1½ cups sugar
½ cup water
2 egg whites
⅛ teaspoon salt
2 tablespoons sherry (or 1 teaspoon vanilla)
3 cups heavy cream, whipped
Candied cherries and angelica for garnish

Mix the sugar and water together in a saucepan and
boil until the syrup comes to 230°-234°—or spins a
thread when dropped from a spoon. Whip the egg
whites with the salt until stiff and pour the hot syrup
over them in a slow stream, beating constantly. When
the mixture is cool, add the vanilla or sherry, then fold
in the whipped cream. Freeze in a melon-shaped mold.
Turn out on a silver tray and decorate with the candied
cherries and angelica.

*Solid pudding is
better than empty
praise*
ENGLISH PROVERB

Delicately-flavored custards are popular desserts all over Europe. Italian *crema*, Spanish *flan* or French *crème*, all are rich in cream and eggs. Here are two worthy variations.

CRÈME BRÛLÉE *(Burnt Cream)*

> 3 cups heavy cream
> 1″ piece of vanilla bean
> 6 egg yolks
> 6 tablespoons sugar
> ½ cup brown sugar (or more)

Scald the cream with the vanilla bean in the top of a double boiler. Beat the egg yolks with the 6 tablespoons sugar until light and creamy.

Discard the vanilla bean and pour the warm cream into the egg yolk mixture gradually, stirring all the time. Return to the double boiler and heat over boiling water, stirring constantly until the mixture coats the spoon. Pour into a pyrex glass serving dish, cool, and refrigerate until set.

At serving time, cover the top of the custard completely with brown sugar, ½ cup or more, so that none of the custard shows through. Place the dish in a bowl of cracked ice and run it under the flame of the broiler until the sugar melts and carmelizes. Watch carefully, as the sugar burns easily. Serve at once.

CRÈME RENVERSÉE AU CARAMEL

> 1 cup cream
> 1 cup milk
> 1″ piece of vanilla bean
> 3 eggs
> 2 egg yolks
> ½ cup sugar
> Additional 1 cup sugar for caramel sauce
> ½ cup water

Scald the milk and cream together with the vanilla bean. Beat the eggs and egg yolks till fluffy, gradually adding the ½ cup of sugar as you continue beating.

Discard the vanilla bean and gradually pour the hot

milk mixture into the egg mixture, stirring constantly. Heat the 1 cup of sugar in a heavy skillet over a moderate flame until it melts. Add the water a little at a time, and stir until brown and well-blended. Pour the caramel into a ring mold, turning it until the entire inside is well coated. When the caramel is set, pour the custard into the mold and set in a pan of hot water. Bake at 350° about 45 minutes, or until a knife inserted in the center comes out clean. Cool, then unmold onto a serving plate.

ZABAGLIONE

When Catharine de Medici went to France in 1533 to marry Henry II, she brought with her a staff of Florentine cooks, thus introducing the finest of Renaissance cooking to the country that was later to be famous for its cuisine. The French eagerly accepted this winey Italian custard and in time produced their own version, Sauce Sabayon (see Chapter VIII).

This recipe appears in Bartolomeo Stefani's *L'Arte di Ben Cucinare* (1662).

> **6 egg yolks**
> **2 tablespoons sugar**
> **6 tablespoons Marsala wine**

Put the egg yolks in the top of a double boiler and beat with a whisk or electric beater until foamy. Gradually add the sugar as you continue beating.

Bring 1 inch of water in the bottom of the double boiler to a simmer and place the pan with the egg yolk mixture over it. Do not let the water touch the bottom of the pan, or go beyond a simmer. Add the wine and continue beating until triple in volume and thick and hot.

Traditionally Zabaglione is served hot in parfait glasses, but it may also be used as a sauce for fruit.

To make cold Zabaglione, pour the hot mixture into a bowl set into another bowl of cracked ice. Beat vigorously until cold and chill until ready to serve.

This dish may be prepared in a chafing dish at the table, if more drama is wanted.

THE CULINARY *art
follows diplomacy
and every prime
minister is its
tributary.*
CAREME

The chafing dish lends an aura of romance and drama to all dishes, even the simplest. Usually associated with the elegance of Victorian times, it is really a very ancient utensil. Chafing dishes were discovered in the ruins of Pompeii.

BANANAS AU RHUM

> **2 tablespoons butter**
> **2 bananas**
> **brown sugar**
> **cinnamon**
> **2 ounces warm rum**

Melt the butter in the top pan, or blazer, of the chafing dish. When it is hot, place in it 2 bananas, peeled and sliced in half lengthwise. Sprinkle with sugar and cinnamon and sauté until lightly browned. Turn and sauté the other side, sprinkling again with sugar and cinnamon.. When the bananas are soft, but not mushy, pour over 2 ounces of warmed rum and ignite. Serve immediately.

CHERRIES JUBILEE

> **6 tablespoons red currant jelly**
> **3 cups canned pitted black cherries**
>   **(juice drained off)**
> **⅔ cup cognac**
> **4 tablespoons cherry juice**
> **1 quart vanilla ice cream, formed in balls**
>   **and frozen hard**

Melt jelly in chafing dish over direct heat, add pitted cherries and juice. When heated pour in warm cognac and blaze. Serve over ice cream. Serves 6.

CRÊPES SUZETTE

This classic sweet pancake was created for Edward, Prince of Wales, by Henri Charpentier while he was still a lowly assistant waiter at the Café de Paris in Monte Carlo. The crêpes were promptly named for a lady in the Prince's party.

Zuppa Inglese, a delicious Italian joke

CRÊPES SUZETTE

2 egg yolks
2 whole eggs
1 cup flour
pinch of salt
1 tablespoon sugar
1½ cups milk (approximate)
2 tablespoons Kirsch

Beat egg yolks and whole eggs together. Sift the flour with the sugar and salt. Stir flour mixture gradually into the eggs. Add milk slowly, using as much as needed to make a smooth batter that is the thickness of cream. Add Kirsch and refrigerate the batter for about an hour.

Butter a small frying pan 5 or 6″ in diameter, and heat till very hot. Pour in about 2 tablespoons of the batter, moving the pan to spread the batter evenly over the bottom. Cook till edges appear brown, then turn to brown the other side. If the crêpes are too thick, add a little milk to the batter; if too thin and difficult to turn, add a little flour.

Remove the crêpes to a platter and continue baking till all are done. This makes about 20 crêpes. Crêpes may be made ahead of time and brought to the table on a heated platter when the guests are ready for dessert.

SAUCE FOR CREPES

4 lumps sugar
juice of 1 orange
1 teaspoon lemon juice
2 tablespoons butter
2 tablespoons Curacao
2 tablespoons Grand Marnier
2 tablespoons Cognac (warmed)

Rub the sugar lumps against the skin of an orange and crush them in the top pan of the chafing dish. Add lemon juice and butter and mix well. Pour in orange juice, Curacao and Grand Marnier and bring to a boil. Put the cooked crêpes in the sauce, one by one, and turn so each is saturated. Fold in quarters like a handkerchief and push to the side. When all the crêpes are sauced and folded, sprinkle them with the warmed cognac. Set ablaze and baste the crêpes till the fire dies out.

COFFEE JELLY

> 2 ounces gelatin
> ¾ cup cold water
> 2 ounces Kahlua
> 2¾ cups fresh hot coffee
> ⅔ cup sugar
> dash salt
> ½ recipe Crème Chantilly for Decorating
>   (Chapter VIII)

Soften gelatin in cold water. Add the hot coffee, sugar and salt. Stir till dissolved. Cool, then stir in Kahlua. Pour into a mold and chill in refrigerator till set. Unmold on a platter and garnish with the Crème Chantilly. Force the Crème from a pastry bag with a star tube, making a fancy border and decorative rosettes.

The flavor mellows and ripens, if kept overnight in the refrigerator.

SHERRY JELLY

> 2 ounces gelatin
> ½ cup cold water
> 1 cup boiling water
> ¾ cup sugar
> ¼ teaspoon salt
> ½ cup orange juice
> 2 tablespoons lemon juice
> 1½ cups sherry
> (use a medium-sweet, gold-colored sherry)
> ½ recipe Crème Chantilly for Decorating
>   (Chapter VIII)

Soften gelatin in cold water. Add boiling water, sugar and salt. Stir till dissolved. Add fruit juices and sherry. Pour into small fancy molds or sherbet glasses. Chill in refrigerator till set. Garnish with rosettes of the Crème Chantilly.

CHAPTER III

AMERICAN HERITAGE DESSERTS

Take almost any American out of his native land and it's not too long before he develops a craving for a piece of good old-fashioned chocolate cake, fresh apple pie or strawberry shortcake with thick rich cream.

These American desserts remind us of youth and home, of the good life in a land of abundance. They are simple, satisfying and unadorned, with direct and honest flavors that come from the good ingredients themselves.

The American desserts that seem most traditional to us come from the hearty farm cooking of the 19th century, when most people lived in rural communities . . . a time when most of what graced the table was the product of their own labor and skill. Here are some of the best of these desserts.

STRAWBERRY SHORTCAKE

Outstanding because of the delicious contrasts of color, texture, flavor and temperature. An American classic!

> 1 **quart strawberries, hulled, cleaned and slightly crushed with a wire potato masher, sweetened to taste**
> 1¾ **cups sifted flour**
> 3 **teaspoons baking powder**
> ½ **teaspoon salt**
> 3 **tablespoons sugar**
> 4 **tablespoons chilled butter**
> ¾ **cup rich milk**
> 1 **cup heavy cream, whipped**
> **whole berries for garnish**

Chill the crushed berries. Combine the dry ingredients and sift into a bowl, cut in butter with a pastry blender until mixture is the texture of coarse corn meal. Make a well in the center, pour in the milk, and stir lightly until just blended. Put into a buttered loaf pan and bake at 400° for about 20 minutes, or until done.

Cut into 8 slices with a cake breaker while still warm. For each serving, lay a slice on a plate, butter generously, top with a heaping tablespoonful of chilled berries, cover with another slice and more berries. Finish with a puff of whipped cream and a whole berry. Serves 4.

INDIAN PUDDING (*Hasty Pudding*)

Maize, or corn meal, the gift of the American Indians to the Pilgrims, is the important ingredient of this delicious pudding. A hearty dessert for a winter evening.

> ⅓ **cup yellow corn meal**
> ⅓ **cup cold water**

1 quart milk
½ teaspoon salt
½ teaspoon cinnamon
1 teaspoon ginger
¾ cup dark molasses
¼ cup butter

Stir corn meal and water together. Scald the milk and stir in the corn meal mixture. Cook over very low heat, stirring constantly, for about 20 minutes or until thick. Add the rest of the ingredients and mix well. Pour into a buttered 1½ quart casserole and bake in a 325° oven about one and a half to two hours.

New Englanders serve this pudding with ice cream. It is also good with cream.

GEORGIA NUT BREAD

A centuries-old recipe from this great nut-producing state. It is rich and sweet enough for tea-time or dessert.

2 eggs
1 cup dark brown sugar, firmly packed
4 cups sifted flour
4 teaspoons baking powder
½ teaspoon salt
2 cups milk
1 cup finely chopped pecans

Combine eggs and brown sugar; beat until sugar is dissolved. Sift flour, baking powder and salt together. Add flour mixture alternately with milk to egg mixture. Stir in pecans. Pour into two well-buttered 9″ x 5″ loaf pans. Cover pans and let stand 30 minutes before baking. Bake at 350° for 45 to 50 minutes or until golden brown. Cool on wire racks 15 minutes. Remove bread from pans; cool thoroughly before slicing.

FAME *at best an unperforming cheat; But 'tis substantial happiness to eat.*
POPE

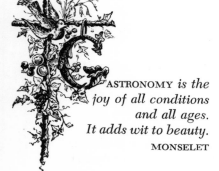

ASTRONOMY *is the joy of all conditions and all ages. It adds wit to beauty.*
MONSELET

APPLE PIE

Certainly pie is the most popular American dessert, and apple pie is the champion of all.

> 1 recipe Pastry for Pies (Chapter VII)
> 6 medium-size, tart cooking apples
> ⅛ teaspoon salt
> 1 tablespoon corn starch
> ½ teaspoon cinnamon
> ½ to ¾ cup sugar (depending on the tartness of apples)
> 2 tablespoons butter

Peel, core and thinly slice the apples. Combine the salt, cornstarch, cinnamon and sugar and sift over the apples. Stir them gently, so that each slice is coated. Fit half of the pie crust into a 9″ pie tin and fill with the apples. Cover with the remaining pie crust and slash the crust in a decorative design. Flute edges. Bake at 450° for 10 minutes, reduce heat to 350° and bake an additional 35 or more minutes, or until apples are tender and crust golden brown. Serve warm with slices of aged cheddar cheese, cream or vanilla ice cream.

CUSTARD PIE

> ½ recipe Pastry for Pies (Chapter VII)
> 3 eggs
> ½ cup sugar
> ¼ teaspoon salt
> 1 teaspoon vanilla
> 2½ cups milk

Separate one of the eggs, reserve yolk. Beat the egg white until stiff, add the sugar, salt and vanilla. Beat the reserved egg yolk and the other two eggs slightly. Blend with the egg white mixture. Warm the milk, pour it into the egg mixture and blend again. Pour into the pie shell.

Place in a preheated 450° oven and immediately turn down the heat to 425°. Bake *exactly* 30 minutes. Should a soft spot remain in the center of the pie, it is an aesthetic defect only. The flavor will be fine.

PERFECT LEMON PIE

An old-fashioned pie that surpasses any of its modern variations.

> ½ recipe Pastry for Pies (Chapter VII)
> 1 cup sugar
> 6 tablespoons corn starch
> ⅛ teaspoon salt
> 2 cups water
> 3 beaten egg yolks
> 3 tablespoons butter
> ⅓ cup fresh lemon juice
> 2 teaspoons coarsely-grated lemon rind

Bake a one crust pie shell with fluted edge. Cool.

Mix the sugar, corn starch and salt in a heavy saucepan and pour in the water. Cook over low heat, stirring constantly until mixture thickens and becomes clear. Pour a little of the mixture into the egg yolks, blend quickly and pour back into the mixture in the saucepan. Cook and stir over the lowest heat for 3 minutes. Remove from heat and beat in the butter, lemon juice and rind. Cool and pour into the pie shell. Cover with meringue, sealing edges well and bake at 350° for about 18 minutes, or until very delicately browned. Cool for several hours before serving.

MERINGUE
> 3 egg whites
> 6 tablespoons sugar
> ⅛ teaspoon salt

Beat the egg whites with the salt until stiff. Fold in the sugar gradually.

THE MOST *indispensable quality of a cook is exactitude: It should also be that of the guest.*
BRILLAT-SAVARIN

FRESH CHERRY PIE

> 1 recipe Pastry for Pies (Chapter VII)
> 4 cups fresh sour cherries, pitted
> 1⅓ cups sugar (or to taste)
> 2 drops almond extract
> 2 teaspoons quick-cooking tapioca
> 4 tablespoons flour
> 2 tablespoons butter

Put the cherries in a large bowl. Mix the sugar, flour and tapioca and sprinkle over the fruit. Add the almond extract. Mix gently. Let stand 15 minutes or more while you prepare the pastry. Fit a 9″ pie tin with ½ the pastry. Cut the remaining rolled pastry into ½ inch strips. Fill the lined pie tin with the cherry mixture, dot with butter.

Make a lattice of the pastry strips over the top of the pie, sealing with cold water at the edges. Bake at 450° for 10 minutes, reduce heat to 350° and bake about 35 minutes more or until crust is golden brown. (A piece of foil placed under the pie tin as it bakes will prevent oven cleanup from the juice boiling over!) Serve warm with cream or vanilla ice cream.

PECAN PIE

This crunchy, deliciously rich dessert is a specialty of the Southern states where pecan trees flourish.

> ½ recipe Pastry for Pies (Chapter VII)
> 4 eggs
> 2 cups dark corn syrup
> ¼ cup melted butter
> 1 teaspoon vanilla
> 1½ cups shelled whole pecans

Line a pie tin with the pastry, building up a high fluted rim. *Do not* prick. Chill. Butter the underside of another pie tin of the same size and set it gently in the pastry shell. (This prevents the shell from buckling.) Bake in a 400° oven for 8 minutes, remove the empty pie tin and allow the shell to cool.

Beat the eggs with a whisk till fluffy, slowly add the syrup, still beating, and mix well. Beat in the melted butter, vanilla and salt, then the pecans. Pour into the pastry shell. Bake at 400° for 35 minutes, or until filling is set. Cool to room temperature before serving.

KEY LIME PIE

This has the true tangy flavor of the Florida fruit.

> ½ recipe Pastry for Pies (Chapter VII)
> ½ cup butter
> 1 cup sugar
> 2 teaspoons grated lime rind
> ½ cup plus 1 tablespoon fresh lime juice
> 4 eggs, beaten
> 1 cup heavy cream, whipped

Bake the Pastry in a 9″ pie tin and cool. Put the butter, sugar, lime rind and juice in the top of a double boiler. Stir in the eggs. Place over boiling water and cook, stirring constantly until thick, about 10 minutes. Cool. Pour into the baked pie shell and chill for about six hours. Spread with whipped cream and serve. Lime pie, contrary to expectations, is not green, but yellow. You may add a few drops of green food coloring if you wish.

MINCE PIE

While mince pie is thought of as being typically American, it was one of the recipes brought over from England by the early settlers of America. As far back as the fourth century spices and liquors were used to preserve meat. Francis Bacon wrote, "Mincing of meat saveth the grinding of the teeth." For a time the Puritans decried mince pies, thinking they had an allusion to the Magi's gifts to the Christ child.

Since the early years of the republic, provident housewives have been "putting up" their own version of mincemeat, often using venison brought in by the hunter, to serve in steaming pies at holiday time. Modern refrigeration has obviated the need for preserving the meat with liquor and spice, but homemade mince meat is such a treat it is well worth while making today.

> 1 recipe Pastry for Pies
> 1½ cups drained mincemeat
> 1¼ cups peeled, chopped tart apples

Line a pie tin with half of the pastry. Mix the apples and mincemeat and put into the pastry shell. Cover with the remaining pastry, first making a decorative design of slits with a small knife to allow steam to escape. Bake at 450° for 30 minutes or until brown. Serve warm with Brandy Hard Sauce or Hot Rum Sauce (Chapter VIII).

MINCEMEAT FILLING

It is impossible to make a small amount of mincemeat, but you will be glad to have jars of it on hand, so mince pies can be produced quickly at any time.

Nothing *more excellent or valuable than wine was ever granted by the gods to man.*

PLATO

4 pounds lean beef
1 pound beef suet
4 cups seedless raisins
4 cups seeded raisins
2 cups currants
1 cup diced citron
1 cup diced orange peel
½ cup diced lemon peel
1 cup chopped figs (optional)
2½ cups sugar
2 teaspoons salt
2 teaspoons nutmeg
2 teaspoons cinnamon
2 teaspoons allspice
1 teaspoon cloves
5 cups cognac or other brandy (approximate)
4 cups sherry (approximate)

Cut the meat in chunks and simmer for about an hour and a half, or until tender, in just enough water to cover. Cool and grind through the coarse blade of a meat grinder. Grind the suet.

Mix well with all the remaining ingredients except cognac and sherry. Add enough cognac to make a thick, soupy mixture. Place in an earthenware container, cover and let stand at least one month. Check in a week to see if mixture seems dry. If it has absorbed most of the liquid, moisten it with sherry. Then check every two weeks, adding alternately cognac or sherry as the mincemeat absorbs the moisture. It will keep indefinitely without refrigeration, but after six weeks or so, you may seal it in glass jars. Makes about 9 quarts.

T HE TABLE *is the only*
place where one
is not bored during
the first hour.
BRILLAT-SAVARIN

FRESH PUMPKIN PIE

Anyone who has ever eaten a pie made with fresh pumpkin will never be content with one made with the canned variety of pumpkin.

  ½ recipe Pastry for Pies (Chapter VII)
  ¾ cup brown sugar
  ½ teaspoon salt
  ¾ teaspoon cinnamon
  ¼ teaspoon ginger
  ¼ teaspoon cloves
  ¼ teaspoon nutmeg
 1½ cups prepared fresh pumpkin
 1½ cups rich milk
  2 beaten eggs
  1 tablespoon dark molasses
  2 tablespoons rum

Prepare the pie crust in a 9″ pie tin, building up a fluted rim. Chill, do not bake. Combine the brown sugar, salt and spices, add remaining ingredients and mix well. Pour into the chilled pie shell. Bake at 450° for 15 minutes, then lower heat to 325° for an additional 30 minutes, or until a knife inserted in the center comes out clean. Serve with Whipped Cream or Vanilla ice cream.

HOW TO PREPARE PUMPKIN FOR FILLING

Wash a medium-size pumpkin and cut in half. Scrape out seeds and strings and place skin-side up in a large baking pan. Bake at 325° for an hour or more until it is tender. Scrape out pulp and put through a sieve or potato ricer.

STEAMED CARROT PUDDING

An inexpensive and delightful winter dessert, festive enough for company and simple enough for children who eat their carrots in this form with virtuous delight.

> ½ cup butter
> 1 cup sugar
> 2 cups finely chopped or ground carrots
> 1 cup finely chopped tart apples
> 2 cups sifted flour
> 1 teaspoon nutmeg
> ½ teaspoon cloves
> 1 teaspoon cinnamon
> 1 teaspoon baking soda
> 1 teaspoon vanilla
> 1 cup raisins (or 1 cup chopped dates)

Cream the butter until fluffy, add sugar gradually and cream again. Stir in the carrots and apples, mix well. Mix the flour with the other dry ingredients, resift and add to the carrot-apple mixture. Mix well. Stir in the vanilla and raisins (or dates).

Pour into well-buttered pudding molds, filling only ⅔ full, cover and seal the cover with butter. Place the molds on trivets in a steamer or heavy kettle. Pour in boiling water. The water should come three quarters of the way up the sides of the molds. Cover the kettle or steamer tightly and steam at low heat for an hour and a half. Serve warm with cream, Brandy Hard Sauce or Custard Sauce (Chapter VIII).

This pudding may be frozen, then reheated by steaming as before.

*IT's food too
fine for angels;
Yet come, take
And eat thy fill! It's
Heaven's Sugar Cake.*
EDWARD TAYLOR

ANGEL FOOD CAKE

Generations of American cooks have had as their goal the achievement of the perfect Angel Food. Here is an old recipe that produces a cake so light it seems to float off the fork!

Only a few precautions are in order. Make sure the eggs are as fresh as possible. Separate the eggs while they are cold, then allow them to come to room temperature before beating. And be sure there is no vestige of grease in the tube pan you are using.

> 1½ cups egg whites (12 or more)
> 2½ tablespoons cold water
> 1½ teaspoons cream of tartar
> 1 teaspoon vanilla
> 1 teaspoon almond extract
> ½ teaspoon salt
> ⅞ cup sifted flour
> 1½ cups sifted fine granulated sugar

Combine the egg whites, water, cream of tartar, vanilla, almond extract and salt. Blend well. Beat with an egg beater or electric mixer just until stiff and still glossy. Fold in, 2 tablespoons at a time, *one* cup of the sugar.

Combine the flour with the other half cup of sugar, then sift six times. Lightly fold the flour mixture into the egg white mixture, a little at a time, using a rubber scraper. Pour into an unbuttered 10″ tube pan. Circle a knife through the batter several times to eliminate any air bubbles. Bake in a 375° oven for 15 minutes, reduce the heat to 250° and bake about 20 minutes more, or until done. Invert the cake till it is cold, then remove it from the pan and glaze with a **Confectioners' Sugar Glaze** (Chapter VIII). Acknowledge applause.

STRAWBERRY ANGEL FOOD CAKE

1 fresh Angel Food cake
2 cups heavy cream
4 tablespoons sugar
1 teaspoon vanilla
1 cup fresh strawberries, sliced and sweetened
    to taste
whole strawberries for garnish

Whip the cream until stiff. Fold in the sugar and vanilla. Slice the cake in two horizontally. Fold the sliced berries into half of the whipped cream and fill the two layers. Ice the cake with the remainder of the sweetened whipped cream and garnish with the perfect whole berries.

BOURBON POUND CAKE

1 pound butter
3 cups sugar
8 eggs, separated
3 cups sifted flour
3 teaspoons baking powder
2 teaspoons vanilla
2 teaspoons almond extract
½ cup bourbon
½ cup chopped pecans

Cream butter and 2 cups sugar together till light and fluffy. Add egg yolks, one at a time, beating thoroughly after each. Add flour alternately with flavoring and bourbon in thirds, beating smooth after each addition. Beat egg whites until stiff but not dry. Beat remaining sugar gradually into egg whites. Fold egg white mixture gently into egg yolk-butter mixture. Sprinkle nuts in bottom of well-buttered 10″ tube pan. Carefully pour batter over nuts in pan. Bake at 350° for 90 minutes or until done.

73

Mʏ ᴍᴀɴɴᴇʀ *of living is plain: a glass of wine and a bit of mutton are always ready, and such as are content to partake of that are always welcome.*
ɢᴇᴏʀɢᴇ ᴡᴀsʜɪɴɢᴛᴏɴ

MARY BALL WASHINGTON'S GINGERBREAD (1784)

The recipe for this rich, spicy cake was found in an old worn cookbook belonging to the mother of our first president.

> ½ cup butter
> ½ cup dark brown sugar, firmly packed
> ½ cup light molasses
> ½ cup honey
> ¼ cup sherry
> ½ cup warm milk
> 3 cups sifted flour
> 2 tablespoons ground ginger
> 1½ teaspoons ground cinnamon
> 1½ teaspoons ground mace
> 1½ teaspoons ground nutmeg
> 1 teaspoon cream of tartar
> 3 eggs, well beaten
> 2 tablespoons grated orange rind
> ¼ cup orange juice
> 1 cup sultanas or raisins
> 1 teaspoon baking soda
> 2 tablespoons warm water

Cream butter until light. Add brown sugar and cream again. Add molasses, honey, sherry and milk. Beat very well. Sift flour, ginger, cinnamon, mace, nutmeg and cream of tartar together. Add alternately with beaten eggs to sugar mixture. Add orange rind and juice, raisins and baking soda dissolved in warm water. Pour into a buttered 13″ x 9″ pan lined with buttered wax paper. Bake 45 to 50 minutes in a 350° oven until cake is firm in center. Cut into squares. Makes 12 servings.

Pineapple Upside-Down Cake

CHOCOLATE PEPPERMINT CAKE

A very pretty, well-flavored cake that was sometimes called "Silhouette Cake." Don't attempt to make it in hot, humid weather, unless your house is air-conditioned.

  1¾ cups sifted flour
    1 teaspoon baking soda
  ¼ teaspoon salt
  ¾ cup butter
  1¼ cups light brown sugar
    3 eggs
    1 teaspoon vanilla
    4 ounces unsweetened chocolate, melted
      and cooled
  ¾ cup water
    1 recipe Seven Minute Icing (Chapter VIII),
      peppermint flavored
    2 ounces unsweetened chocolate, melted
      and cooled

Cream the butter, add sugar gradually and cream again until fluffy. Add the eggs, one at a time, beating well after each addition. Add the vanilla and 4 ounces of chocolate, mix well.

Mix the flour with the baking soda and salt and sift together. Add to the batter, alternately with the water, stirring just enough to blend thoroughly. Pour into two 8″ layer pans that have been buttered and dusted with flour. Bake at 350° for 25 to 30 minutes. Cool.

Fill and ice the top and sides of the cake with the Seven Minute Icing. When the icing has set, pour the 2 ounces of melted chocolate over the top of the cake, spreading it with a spatula, and allowing it to run down the sides of the cake in decorative "dribbles."

I F A MAN *will be sensible and one fine morning while he is lying in bed count at the tips of his fingers how many things in this life truly give him enjoyment, invariably he will find food is the first one.*

LIN YUTANG

LINCOLN LOG

A delicious cake, very similar to the French *Bûche de Noël*, but unmistakably American.

> **1 recipe Chocolate Sponge Sheet (Chapter VII)**
> **Cocoa (as needed)**
> **1 recipe sweetened whipped cream (see Crème Chantilly, Chapter VIII)**
> **1 recipe Uncooked Chocolate Butter Icing (Chapter VIII)**
> **Maraschino cherries for garnish**

Bake the sponge sheet in an 8″ x 16″ pan, and as soon as it is taken out of the oven, invert it on a tea towel sprinkled with cocoa. Do not remove wax paper. Roll the cake as tightly as possible in the towel to a 16″-long cylinder. Cool, carefully unroll and peel off the wax paper. Trim off the crusty edges, spread thickly with the whipped cream, and roll again. Ice with the Uncooked Chocolate Butter Icing. Run the tines of a fork lightly down the length of the "log" to simulate bark and garnish with cherries placed along the top.

PINEAPPLE REFRIGERATOR CAKE

Refrigerator cakes are an American invention and this is absolutely the most delicious version. Men especially love it.

> **½ pound vanilla wafers**
> **½ cup butter**
> **1½ cups confectioners' sugar**
> **2 eggs**
> **1 9-ounce can crushed pineapple, drained**
> **1 cup heavy cream**

Grind the wafers or roll them into crumbs and put ½ of them in the bottom of an 8″ x 12″ pan. Cream butter and sugar. Add eggs one at a time and beat until smooth and creamy. Pour this mixture over the crumbs. Whip cream, add the pineapple and pour over the first mixture. Cover with the rest of the crumbs, pat gently with your hands and refrigerate over night or longer.

GERMAN SWEET CHOCOLATE CAKE

> 4 ounces Baker's German Sweet Chocolate
> ½ cup boiling water
> 1 cup butter
> 2 cups sugar
> 4 unbeaten egg yolks
> 2¼ cups sifted flour
> ½ teaspoon salt
> 1 teaspoon baking soda
> 1 cup buttermilk
> 4 egg whites beaten stiff
> 1 recipe Coconut Pecan Icing (Chapter VIII)

Melt chocolate in boiling water, cool. Cream butter and sugar till fluffy, add egg yolks, one at a time, beat well after each. Add melted chocolate mixture and vanilla, mix well. Sift together flour, salt and soda. Add alternately with buttermilk to chocolate mixture, beating after each addition till smooth. Carefully fold in beaten egg whites. Bake in two 9″ layer cake pans at 350° for 40 to 45 minutes. Fill and ice the top with Coconut Pecan Icing.

APPLE DUMPLINGS

> 2 recipes Pastry for Pies (Chapter VII)
> 6 medium size baking apples
> ¾ cup firmly packed brown sugar
> 1 teaspoon cinnamon
> ⅓ cup chopped nuts
> 2 tablespoons lemon juice
> 3 tablespoons butter

Roll pastry ⅛″ thick and cut into 6 squares. Peel and core apples. Lightly mix brown sugar, cinnamon and chopped nuts. Fill the apples with the sugar mixture. Sprinkle with lemon juice and dot with butter. Bring opposite edges of the pastry together on top of the apples. Moisten edges with water and seal. Make several gashes in each dumpling with a sharp knife to allow steam to escape. Bake in a 375 degree oven about 40 minutes or until apples are tender, and pastry browned. Serve warm with cream or Lemon Sauce (Chapter VIII).

THE UNIVERSE *is*
nothing without life
and all that lives
takes nourishment.
BRILLAT-SAVARIN

LADY BALTIMORE CAKE

A famous old recipe for a superlative dessert.

CAKE:

> 2 cups sugar
> 1 cup butter
> 3⅛ cups sifted flour
> 4 teaspoons baking powder
> ½ teaspoon salt
> 1 cup milk
> 1 teaspoon vanilla
> ¼ teaspoon almond extract
> 8 egg whites
> ⅛ teaspoon salt

Sift the sugar. Cream the butter till fluffy, add the sugar gradually and cream again till very light and fluffy. Mix the flour, baking powder and ½ teaspoon salt together, sift twice. Add the flour mixture to the butter mixture in 3 parts, alternately with thirds of milk, stirring till smooth after each addition. Stir in the vanilla and almond extract.

Beat the egg whites with the ⅛ teaspoon of salt till stiff but not dry. Fold gently into the batter. Bake in 3 buttered 8″ layer cake pans at 350° for about 25 minutes.

FILLING AND ICING:

> 2 recipes Seven Minute Icing (Chapter VIII)
> ½ cup chopped figs
> ½ cup chopped pecans
> 1 cup chopped raisins
> Whole pecans for decoration

Make the icing and reserve two-thirds of it. Fold the

figs, pecans and raisins into the remaining third and use to fill the layers. Ice the top and sides of the cake with the reserved icing and decorate the top with the whole pecans.

PINEAPPLE UPSIDE-DOWN CAKE
Photograph page 76

Pretty, easy to make and a long-time favorite.

TOPPING:
> ½ cup butter
> 1 cup brown sugar
> 8 or 9 canned pineapple slices
> 8 or 9 candied cherries

Drain the pineapple, reserve juice. Melt the butter in a large skillet. Spread the brown sugar over the butter and arrange the pineapple slices on top. Put a cherry in each pineapple slice hole.

CAKE BATTER:
> 3 eggs, separated
> 1 cup sugar
> 5 tablespoons pineapple juice
> ⅞ cup sifted flour
> 1 teaspoon baking powder
> ⅛ teaspoon salt

Beat the egg yolks till light and fluffy and beat in the sugar. Sift the flour with the salt and baking powder and fold into the egg yolk mixture, alternately with the pineapple juice. Gently fold in the stiffly-beaten egg whites. Pour the batter over the pineapple in the skillet.
Bake in a 375° oven for about 25 to 30 minutes. Turn out onto a serving plate and serve warm with whipped cream or vanilla ice cream.

HE WHO *receives his friends and gives no personal attention to the meal prepared for them is unworthy of having friends.*
BRILLAT-SAVARIN

APPLE SAUCE LOAF

An old-fashioned spicy cake that's very good served plain, perhaps with fruit or ice cream, or iced with Uncooked Bittersweet Chocolate Icing or Caramel Icing (Chapter VIII). It's moist enough to keep well for several days, but it's so delicious you'll have a hard time saving it from eager nibblers!

> 1¾ cups sifted flour
> 1 teaspoon baking powder
> ½ teaspoon soda
> ¼ teaspoon salt
> 1 teaspoon cinnamon
> ½ teaspoon cloves
> ½ cup soft butter
> 1 cup sugar
> 1 egg well beaten
> ¾ cup applesauce

Mix all dry ingredients together and sift. Cream butter thoroughly, gradually add the sugar and cream again till light and fluffy. Add egg and mix well. Add the flour mixture alternately with the applesauce, beating till smooth, after each addition. Pour into a buttered 9″ x 5″ loaf pan and bake in a 350° oven about an hour, or until cake pulls away from sides of pan.

You may fold in 1 cup of chopped nuts and 1 cup of chopped, lightly floured raisins after adding the applesauce and flour mixture.

CHAPTER IV

LITTLE TREASURES

It's true. Often the best things *do* come in small packages. The tiny tartlet has an appeal that even the grandest tarte cannot match. And the dainty petit four can be even more irresistible than the most decorative torte.

These little pastries need not be reserved for desserts. A few Madeleines, Langues du Chat or Amaretti with a glass of wine are civilizing refreshments at any time from "high tea" to the late evening snack. A handful of sugar cookies and cold milk will do much to restore morning energies. And, of course, any of the confections in this chapter will serve very nicely to revive that charming institution of Afternoon Tea—the welcome break in routine when friends gather for an assortment of delicious tid-bits accompanied by hot tea, coffee or (as in Vienna) *Schokolade mit schlag*. A perfect setting for relaxing conversation.

WHEN *there is no more cookery in the world, there will be no more letters, no quick and lofty intelligence, no pleasant and easy relationships; no more social unity.*

CAREME

MADELEINES
Photograph page 94

Delicate shell-shaped little cakes, said by some historians to have been invented by Talleyrand's great pastry-chef, Avice. Others say they were well known in France long before his time, having first been made in Commercy, where they are still a gastronomic specialty. This recipe follows as closely as possible that of the pastry-makers of Commercy.

> 4 eggs
> 1½ cups sugar
> 1 teaspoon grated lemon rind
> 1 teaspoon vanilla
> 2 cups sifted flour
> 1½ cups clarified butter, melted and cooled
>   (Chapter VII)

Mix eggs, sugar and lemon rind in a large bowl until just combined. Set bowl over a pan containing 1 or 2″ of hot water. (Water must not touch bowl.) Place over a very low heat until mixture is just lukewarm. This helps the eggs to whip to much greater volume. Stir them as they are warming, 3 or 4 times to prevent from cooking at the bottom of the bowl. When lukewarm, remove from heat and beat with an electric mixer at high speed for 10 or 15 minutes, or until fluffy and tripled in bulk.

Add vanilla. Gently fold in flour. Then add butter, being careful not to over-mix.

Fill very well-buttered madeleine molds two-thirds full. (It is easier to do this with a pastry tube.) Bake about 10 minutes in a 375° oven or until golden. Remove from molds immediately. Makes about 4 dozen cakes.

Madeleines and a glass of wine make a fine light dessert. Dunking is permitted!

ENGLISH LEMON CHEESE TARTS
Devoid of cheese, but rich in lemon flavor!
>**8 baked tartlet or barquette shells**
>   **(see Chapter VII, Rich Tart Pastry)**
>**1 recipe Lemon Curd (Chapter VIII)**
>**½ recipe Crème Chantilly (Chapter VIII)**
>**Strawberries or glaced cherries for garnish**

Fill the little pastry shells with lemon curd, top each with a puff or rosette of Crème Chantilly and garnish each with a fresh strawberry or cherry. Very pretty on a tea tray or as a dessert for buffet dinner.

CHAUSSONS AUX POMMES *(Apple turnovers)*
>**½ recipe Puff Paste (Chapter VII)**
>**4 tart cooking apples, peeled, cored and**
>   **cut in thin slices**
>**¼ cup sugar (or to taste)**
>**½ cup water**
>**1 piece vanilla bean, 3″ long**
>**2 beaten egg yolks**
>**⅔ cup sliced filberts**

Boil together the sugar, water and vanilla bean for 10 minutes. Add the apple slices, a few at a time and poach until tender. Remove from syrup with a slotted spoon and repeat until all the fruit is used. If the syrup is thin, boil until a thick consistency is reached. Pour the syrup over the apple slices. Cool.

Roll out chilled paste to about ⅛″ thickness and cut in 4″ squares. Moisten the edges of the squares with water and put a little of the apple compote on half of each square. Fold diagonally to form a triangle and pinch the edges together. Place on a buttered baking sheet, chill well. Brush each turnover with the beaten egg yolk, sprinkle with sliced filberts, and bake in a 350° oven about 20 minutes, or until golden.

CANDIED ANGELICA
*Cut your angelica in
lengths when young, and
boil it till it is tender.
Then peel it, put it in again
and let it simmer and
boil till it is green.
Then take it up, dry it
with a cloth, and to every
pound of stalks put a
pound of sugar. Put your
stalks into an earthern
pan, beat your sugar, strew
it over them and let them
stand two days. Then
boil it till it is clear
and green, and put it
in a cullender to drain.
Beat another pound of sugar
to powder, and strew it
over the angelica; then lay
it on plates, and let it
stand in a slack oven till
it is thoroughly dry.*

THE HOUSEKEEPER'S INSTRUCTOR
*or
Universal Family Cook
London circa 1800*

PETITS FOURS GLACÉS

Photograph page 94

These are the elegant and delicious little French cakes that look so impressive on a tea tray, and make a festive light ending to a buffet dinner. Part of their appeal is the variety of their flavors, colors and decorations. It is a real artistic experience to turn out a tray of petits fours!

According to Carême, the cakes were named "Petits Fours", *little ovens*, because they were baked after the big cakes were finished, when the heat of the oven had lessened considerably.

> **CAKE:**
> **Génoise, Almond Butter or Basic Sponge Sheet** (Chapter VII)
>
> **FILLING:**
> **Apricot or raspberry jam** (about 1 cup) **or Continental Butter Cream** (Chapter VIII)
>
> **ICING:**
> **3 cups Wilton Fondant, flavored and tinted as you choose** (Chapter VIII)
>
> **DECORATIONS:**
> **½ cup fondant, candied violets, candied fruits, pistachios, flowers made from Wilton Buttercream** (Chapter VIII)
> **One recipe Apricot Glaze** (Chapter VIII)

Bake the cake in an 11″ x 16″ jelly roll pan. The sheets of cake should be not more than ¾-inch high. The cake will cut more easily if baked a day or two ahead and refrigerated. Cut the cake in half, making two layers, 8″ x 11″, and fill the layers with jam or Continental Butter Cream. Brush the top with hot apricot glaze and trim off all crisp edges. Using a sharp knife, and wiping it frequently, cut the cake into small squares, circles and diamonds. (It's a good idea to plan the cuts on a piece of paper with a ruler to minimize waste.)

Place the small shapes on a wire cake rack over a shallow pan, leaving space between each. Melt the fondant and quickly pour it over the cakes, letting it run down and coat the sides. (Scrape up the excess fondant from the pan to reheat and use again, thinning if necessary.) Allow cakes to dry for about 10 minutes.

Decorate each with scrolls and borders of tinted fondant, piped through a pastry bag fitted with the smallest tube. Or trim with flowers made in advance with Wilton Buttercream and refrigerated. Or use bits of crushed candied violets, candied fruits or pistachios. This recipe makes about 45 petits fours.

OLD-FASHIONED SUGAR COOKIES

Generations of mothers and grandmothers have filled countless cookie jars with these. A cold glass of milk and a few Sugar Cookies make a marvelous snack.

> **½ cup butter**
> **1 cup sugar**
> **1 egg or two egg yolks, well beaten**
> **1 tablespoon milk**
> **½ teaspoon vanilla**
> **1½ cups sifted flour**
> **1 teaspoon baking powder**
> **¼ teaspoon salt**
> **Sugar for garnish**

Cream butter until fluffy. Beat in 1 cup sugar, egg or egg yolks, milk and vanilla. Sift flour, baking powder and salt together. Add to butter mixture. Mix well. Cover. Refrigerate three to four hours or until dough is firm. Form into small balls about ¾ inch in diameter. Place 2 inches apart on buttered cookie sheets. Flatten tops lightly with the bottom of a glass that has been dipped in sugar. Bake 8 to 10 minutes in a 375° oven or until lightly browned around the edges. Cool on wire racks. Makes 3 dozen.

R ECEIPT FOR MAKING
STILTON CHEESE
*Take the night's cream,
and put it to the morning's
new milk, with the rennet;
when the curd is come, it
is not to be broken, as is
done with other cheeses, but
take it out with a soil-
dish altogether, and place
it in the sieve to drain
gradually and, as it drains,
keep gradually pressing
it till it becomes firm and
dry on boards, turned
frequently, with cloth
binders round it, which are
to be tightened as
occasion requires.*
N.B. *The Dairy-maid must
not be disheartened if she
does not succeed perfectly in
the first attempt.*
THE HOUSEKEEPER'S INSTRUCTOR
or
*Universal Family Cook
London circa 1800*

DANISH BUTTER COOKIES

1 cup butter
1 cup sugar
1 egg
2 cups sifted flour
½ teaspoon cream of tartar
½ teaspoon baking soda
Pecans for garnish

Cream shortening and sugar, add egg and beat till fluffy. Sift together dry ingredients and mix into butter mixture thoroughly, a little at a time. Roll into small balls the size of a walnut and place on buttered cookie sheet. Flatten with a fork and garnish each with a pecan half. Bake in a 350° oven eight to ten minutes, till delicately brown on edges.

PETITS CORNETS (*Little Cornucopias*)

1 egg
⅓ cup sugar
2 tablespoons water
1 teaspoon vanilla
½ cup sifted cake flour
Finely chopped toasted almonds for garnish
1 recipe Crème Chantilly (Chapter VIII)

Beat egg slightly in a small deep bowl, add sugar and continue to beat until very fluffy. Gradually add the water, beating in till thick and fluffy. Add the flour all at once, and fold in until just blended.

Drop the batter onto buttered and floured baking sheets, spreading with a spoon to a thin 5″ circle. Bake at 350° for about 10 minutes, or until golden. Remove from baking sheet at once, and roll into a cone while still warm. (It is best to bake only three cookies at a time, so they do not cool before rolling. If cookies become too stiff to roll, return to oven for a moment to soften.) Fill the cornucopias with the Crème Chantilly, and sprinkle with the chopped almonds. Makes 12 cookies.

J ANUARY'S FLOWER
The Snowdrop

VANILLA REFRIGERATOR COOKIES

Rich, delicious little sweets that keep well.

> 1 cup sugar
> ½ cup butter
> 1 egg
> 1 teaspoon vanilla
> ½ teaspoon grated lemon rind
> 1¾ cups sifted flour
> ¼ teaspoon salt
> 2 teaspoons baking powder

Cream the butter till fluffy, add sugar, a little at a time, beat till very light. Beat in egg and lemon rind. Sift the dry ingredients together and stir into the preceding mixture.

Shape the dough into a long roll about 2″ in diameter. (If it is too soft to handle, chill it before shaping. Do not use additional flour.) Roll in wax paper. Chill at least 24 hours. Cut in very thin slices and bake on buttered cookie sheet about 10 minutes in a 400° oven.

BUTTERSCOTCH REFRIGERATOR COOKIES

Substitute 1¼ cups packed brown sugar for the white sugar in Vanilla Refrigerator Cookies.

PINWHEEL COOKIES

> **Dough for Vanilla Refrigerator Cookies**
> **1 ounce unsweetened chocolate**

Melt and cool the chocolate. Divide the dough into two equal parts. Add chocolate to one part and chill both doughs until easy to roll. Roll both the light and brown doughs separately, between sheets of wax paper, into oblongs about ⅛″ thick. Place the dark dough on the light dough and roll up like a jelly roll. Wrap in wax paper and chill 24 hours. Cut in thin slices and bake on a buttered cookie sheet at 400° for about 10 minutes.

F EBRUARY'S FLOWER
The Primrose

CORNETS À LA CRÈME *(Cream Horns)*

½ recipe Puff Paste (Chapter VII)
2 lightly beaten egg yolks
Coarse crystallized sugar
2 recipes Crème Chantilly (Chapter VIII)

You will need metal tubes or horn molds to make cornets. Butter the tubes well.

Roll out the chilled pastry to about ⅛″ thick and cut into long strips ¾″ wide. (A 5½″ tube will need a 30″ long strip.) Starting at the narrowest part of the tube, wind the pastry around it to within ½″ of the top. Slightly overlap the dough as you wind and be careful not to stretch it. Chill the tubes in the refrigerator for several hours, or even freeze them. Brush the tubes with the egg yolks, leaving a 1″ strip clear which will rest on the cookie sheet for baking. Roll the tubes in the sugar and place them on their sides on an unbuttered cookie sheet about 1″ apart.

Bake in a 350° oven for about 40 minutes, or until golden brown. As soon as they are out of the oven, twist them free of the molds and cool on a rack.

Just before serving, fill the horns with the Crème Chantilly, using a pastry bag and tube.

PECAN DROPS

1 pound butter
1 cup sugar
4 cups flour
2 egg yolks
2 teaspoons vanilla
1 pound ground pecans
Confectioners' sugar for dusting

Cream butter until fluffy and add sugar, a little at a time. Add egg yolks and vanilla, mix well. Add flour, mixing well. Then add pecans, mixing all together thoroughly. Drop by teaspoon onto buttered cookie sheets. Bake at 325° about 15 minutes until light brown. Sprinkle with confectioners' sugar while still hot.

M arch's flower
The Violet

LANGUES DU CHAT *(Cat's Tongues)*

These little sweet biscuits derive their name from their shape—long and slender like a cat's tongue.

> ½ cup soft butter
> ½ cup sugar
> ⅛ teaspoon salt
> ½ teaspoon vanilla
> 4 egg whites
> 1 cup flour

Cream the butter, add sugar, a little at a time. Cream till well-blended and add vanilla and salt. Beat in unbeaten egg whites, one at a time. Fold in flour. Press the batter through a medium-sized pastry tube in strips about 3″ long and 1″ apart onto an unbuttered cookie sheet. Bake at 400° until edges are very lightly browned. Remove at once from cookie sheet.

Very good served with champagne or a dessert wine, or with tea or coffee. Well-covered, they will keep for several weeks.

CHOCOLATE DROP COOKIES

A delicious version of a long-time favorite.

> ½ cup butter
> 1 cup sugar
> ¼ teaspoon salt
> 1 egg
> ¾ cup buttermilk
> ½ teaspoon baking soda
> ½ teaspoon vanilla
> ½ cup cocoa
> 1¾ cups sifted flour
> ½ cup chopped walnuts

Cream butter, add sugar and salt, cream again, add egg, mix well. Sift flour with cocoa. Mix buttermilk with soda. Add flour mixture to butter mixture, alternately with buttermilk mixture. Add vanilla. Stir in walnuts. Drop by teaspoon onto buttered cookie sheets about 2″ apart. Bake at 350° about 10 minutes.

AMARETTI *(Macaroons)*

The origin of these little almond cakes is unknown, but they were already famous in the 17th century. Most authorities agree they were invented in Italy and later brought to France.

> ½ **pound almond paste**
> 1 **cup sugar**
> 3 **egg whites**
> ½ **teaspoon vanilla**

Stir the almond paste to soften it and work in two-thirds of the cup of sugar alternately with the egg whites. Add vanilla. The consistency should be a little softer than that of mashed potatoes.

Cover a cookie sheet with white letter paper, and force the mixture through a medium-size pastry tube into rounds 2″ in diameter, spaced 1″ apart. Sprinkle with the rest of the sugar. Bake at 300° for about 20 minutes, until they are delicately browned.

When they are taken out of the oven, cover a cake rack with a damp towel and slide the paper containing the macaroons onto it. In a few minutes they may be easily removed. Store in a covered container.

TINY ROLLA TORTES

> 2 **recipes Swiss Broyage (Chapter VII)**
> 1 **recipe Continental Butter Cream**
>   **(Chapter VIII)**
> 1½ **cups toasted almonds, coarsely chopped**

Shape the Broyage in 2″ circles and bake. Put 3 of the baked cookies together with the Butter Cream, spreading thinly. Do not ice the top. Ice the sides with the Butter Cream and roll the little cakes in the chopped almonds. Fill a pastry bag fitted with a small star tube with the remaining Butter Cream and make a border of rosettes around the top.

These little cakes are most delicious after they have mellowed in the refrigerator a few days.

A PRIL'S FLOWER
The Daisy

Petits Fours Glacés. On the plate: Langues du Chat, Petits Cornets, Madeleines

M AY'S FLOWER
The Hawthorn

PIGNOLINI *(Pine Nut Cookies)*
A traditional sweet from Italy.

½ pound blanched almonds
1¾ cups confectioners' sugar
1 tablespoon vanilla
3 egg whites
¼ cup sugar
½ pound pine nuts
Confectioners' sugar for dusting

Grind almonds and confectioners' sugar together. Add vanilla and grind again to form a smooth paste. Beat egg whites till stiff. Fold and blend into almond paste. Chill in refrigerator for two hours. Add granulated sugar and blend. Spread pine nuts on board. Break off pieces of dough the size of a walnut, roll between palms, then flatten slightly and roll in pine nuts. Bake on buttered and floured cookie sheets in a 350° oven about 12 minutes or until golden. Remove from sheet, cool and dust with confectioners' sugar. Makes about 2 dozen.

MOLASSES COOKIES

4½ cups sifted flour
2 teaspoons soda
3 teaspoons ginger
1 teaspoon salt
1 cup butter
1 cup brown sugar (packed)
2 eggs, beaten
¾ cups molasses
¾ cup sour milk or buttermilk

Cream butter, sugar, add eggs one at a time, beat well. Add dry ingredients. Chill. Roll and cut into round shapes. Bake at 350 degrees for 8 or 10 minutes.

At Christmas time, cut the rolled dough with a gingerbread man cutter. Decorate the baked cookies with colored Wilton Fondant, or Wilton Butter Cream forced through a pastry bag and tube. A delight for children!

J UNE'S FLOWER
The Honeysuckle

DARIOLES *(Cream Tarts)*

The origin of the tart dates back to the Middle Ages. A recipe for "Daryoles" appeared in an English book on cooking in the 1300's.

½ recipe Puff Pastry (Chapter VII)
1 recipe Frangipane Cream (Chapter VIII)

Roll chilled puff pastry very thin and line 12 tartlet pans with it. Extend the pastry ⅛″ above the pans by pushing it gently with your fingers. Fill with Frangipane Cream and bake in a 350° oven about 25 minutes.

BISCOTTI

Crisp anise-scented slices served in Italy at Christmas.

8 cups sifted flour
¼ cup baking powder
1½ cups butter
2¼ cups sugar
12 eggs
1 teaspoon anise flavoring

Cream butter and sugar. Add eggs, one at a time, beating well. Add anise. Sift flour with baking powder. Work in flour mixture, blending well. Form into 6 cylinders, about 2″ thick. Place about 3″ apart on 2 buttered cookie sheets and bake at 375° for about 30 minutes. When cakes are cooled, cut into ½″ slices, place on cookie sheets and toast in a 325° oven, turning to brown other side. Stored in a tightly covered jar these will keep indefinitely.

INDIANER KRAPFEN *(Indian Puffs)*

A true Viennese delight. Its somewhat confused origin concerns a jealous baker named Krapf, whose wife gave undue attention to a Hindu (Indianer) tight rope walker!

1 recipe Basic Sponge Sheet (Chapter VII)
¼ cup cognac
1 cup Apricot Glaze (Chapter VIII)
1 recipe Crème Chantilly, flavored with
    cognac (Chapter VIII)
Clacéd cherries for garnish
Chocolate Glaze

Fill a large pastry bag, fitted with a large plain tube with the Sponge Sheet batter. Press rounds of batter about 1¼″ in diameter onto a well-buttered baking sheet. Make the rounds high as possible. Bake about 12 minutes at 400°. Cool.

With a spoon, scoop out the inside of each shell, cutting through the flat bottom. Brush the inside of each shell with cognac, then with the Apricot Glaze. Fill with Crème Chantilly and put together in pairs to form balls. Put in freezer for 1 hour.

Put the chilled cakes on a rack and pour the Chocolate Glaze over them, covering each completely. Garnish each with a cherry. Makes about 12 puffs.

CHOCOLATE GLAZE:

3 ounces unsweetened chocolate
¾ cup cream
1 cup sugar
¼ cup water
1 tablespoon corn syrup
1 egg, slightly beaten
1 teaspoon vanilla

Mix the chocolate, cream, sugar, water and corn syrup in a heavy saucepan. Cook and stir over low heat until chocolate melts. Raise heat a little and cook without stirring about 5 minutes, or until a little dropped in cold water forms a soft ball. Pour a little of the chocolate mixture into the egg, mix, then pour back into pan. Cook a few minutes longer until mixture becomes thicker. Cool, then add vanilla.

J ULY'S FLOWER
The Water Lily

FUDGE WEDGIES

The most delicious version of Chocolate Brownies. Served with vanilla or chocolate ice cream, they make a fine, filling dessert.

>½ cup butter
>2 eggs
>1 cup sugar
>½ cup sifted flour
>1 ounce unsweetened chocolate, melted
>1 teaspoon vanilla

Cream butter and sugar until light and fluffy. Add eggs and beat thoroughly. Blend in flour. Add chocolate and vanilla, mix well. Pour into a buttered 9″ pie pan. Bake at 350° for about 25 minutes. Cut into 12 wedge-shaped pieces.

CHEWY DATE BARS

>½ cup butter
>1 cup sugar
>2 eggs
>1 teaspoon vanilla
>½ cup sifted flour
>1 cup finely-cut, pitted dates

Heat oven to 350 degrees. Butter and flour a 9″ square pan. Beat butter until light. Add sugar, eggs, and vanilla; beat until well blended. Stir in flour, blend well. Add dates, mix. Spread mixture in prepared pan. Bake 20 to 25 minutes or until golden brown. Cool on wire rack. Cut into bars. Makes 18 bars.

CHRISTMAS COOKIES

>1 pound butter
>1½ cups sugar
>2 eggs
>½ teaspoon vanilla
>About 5 cups flour
>Coarse red and green sugar for garnish

Cream butter, add sugar, a little at a time, beat till fluffy. Add vanilla, mix well. Add eggs, one at a time, beating well after each addition. Mix in flour, blend well. Force mixture thru pastry bag fitted with a medium or large star tube onto a buttered cookie sheet. (It may be necessary to chill the dough before forming the cookies.) Sprinkle with colored sugar. Bake in a 375° oven for 8 to 10 minutes or until delicately brown.

APRICOT CRESCENTS
½ recipe Puff Paste (Chapter VII)
⅔ cup apricot jam
Confectioners' Sugar

Roll out chilled puff paste to about ⅛″ thickness. Trim edges and cut in triangles about 3″ x 3″ x 4½″. Place a scant teaspoon of apricot jam on the widest part of each triangle, and roll toward the point. Place on unbuttered baking sheet and bend into crescent shape. Bake at 350° about 20 minutes, or until golden. Sprinkle with confectioners' sugar. Makes about 24 crescents.

PAPILLONS *(Butterflies)*
½ recipe Puff Paste (Chapter VII)
Granulated sugar
1 egg white
1 teaspoon water

Roll out chilled puff paste ⅛-inch thick, using plenty of sugar instead of flour to prevent sticking to the board. Trim edges and cut into strips 4″ wide. Mix the egg white and water together. Brush the center of each strip with egg white mixture. Stack 4 strips together, sandwich fashion. With a long dowel, about the thickness of a pencil, press firmly along the length of the "sandwich," making an indentation in the center. Fold in half along indentation. Cut into ¼″ slices and place on a baking sheet. Separate ends of each slice slightly. Bake at 350° for about 20 minutes, or until golden. Makes about 24 Papillons.

FRUIT TARTLETS OR BARQUETTES

These little pastries, so tempting for dessert or tea, are made the same as large tarts. Line tartlet or barquette pans with Rich Tart Pastry (Chapter VII), bake, fill and finish in the same way as Tarte aux Abricots, Tarte aux Fraises (page 23) or Tarte aux Pommes (page 33).

CREAM PUFFS and ÉCLAIRS

Cream puffs and éclairs must rate as near-top favorites in anyone's list of desserts. Everyone considers them special treats, and, when they are homemade and crisp, they are irresistable. Bake them according to directions in Chapter VII (Pâte à Chou). Fill with any version of Crème Patissiére, Whipped Cream Sauce or English Lemon Curd. Dust with confectioners' sugar or ice with Fondant or an Uncooked Butter Icing (all Chapter VIII).

PROFITEROLES *(Tiny Cream Puffs)*

A most elegant dessert or tea offering is an assortment of these tiny puffs. Bake, fill and ice them just as for Cream Puffs, above. (See Chapter VII.)

KAFFEE BRANDTEIGKRAPFEN
(Coffee Cream Puffs)

> 1 recipe Pate à chou (Chapter VII)
> 1 recipe Crême Chantilly (Chapter VIII), flavored with freshly-brewed, triple strength coffee
> 1 recipe Wilton Fondant (Chapter VIII), flavored with triple-strength coffee

Shape the pate à chou with a pastry tube into little ovals resembling coffee beans. Bake and fill with the Crême Chantilly and ice with the coffee-flavored fondant.

The Viennese like to serve these little puffs with afternoon coffee and more whipped cream.

CHAPTER V

S I M P L E

S W E E T S

Sometimes there is just no substitute for *something simple*. Then a slice of cold meat is more appealing than *Tournedos Rossini* and a glass of plain iced water is even more satisfying than the first sip of a vintage wine.

These are the desserts that meet the needs of such occasions—unpretentious, wholesome and modestly sweet. Many of them recall childhood pleasures. Hot gingerbread. Vanilla Pudding, Caramel Custard. Has it been a long time since you enjoyed them?

Here is a modest assortment of simple sweets—easy to prepare, nourishing and reminiscent of simpler times.

*1685 recipe
for
Bread Pudding
from*
THE ACCOMPLISHT COOK
or the
ART & MYSTERY
of
COOKERY
Robert May

*Grate four penny loaves
and force them through a
cullender, put them in
a deep dish, and put to
them four eggs, two quarts
of cream, cloves, mace and
some saffron, salt, rose
water, sugar currans, a
pound of beef suet minced
and a pound of dates...*

PERFECT RICE PUDDING

The very best rice pudding, with a rich, caramel-like flavor. If you remember it from childhood, you will be anxious to make it yourself. If you have never tasted it, prepare for a treat! The proportions may seem unusual, and the baking time amazingly long, but there is no more worthwhile occupation for a winter's day than the preparation of this dessert.

> 8 cups milk
> 4 tablespoons rice (not the quick-cooking variety)
> ⅔ cup sugar
> 1 teaspoon salt

Combine all the ingredients and pour into a large oblong baking dish. Bake in a very slow oven, 225°, for about six hours. Stir the mixture every half hour or so until the rice is completely dissolved and the pudding thickened. Toward the end of the baking, you may add ½ cup of currants or raisins, but the flavor is just as fine without them. Serve warm with cream.

BREAD PUDDING

> 2 cups bread cubes (4 or 5 slices)
> ¼ cup raisins
> 2 cups milk
> 3 tablespoons butter
> ⅓ cup sugar
> dash of salt
> 1 teaspoon vanilla
> 2 eggs
> ½ teaspoon nutmeg
> Currant Jelly

MERINGUE

> 2 egg whites
> dash of salt
> 4 tablespoons sugar

Cut the bread into ½″ cubes, crust and all, and place in a well-buttered 1 qt. baking casserole. Sprinkle with the raisins and mix lightly. Scald the milk, and stir into it, while heating, the butter and sugar. Beat the eggs slightly with a fork, add the salt, nutmeg and vanilla and stir into the milk mixture. Pour over the bread cubes. Set casserole in a pan of warm water and bake 1 hr. in a 350° oven, or until knife inserted in center comes out clean. Dot surface with jelly. Beat egg whites till stiff, then add salt and the sugar, a little at a time, beating till smooth and glossy. Spread over pudding and bake in a 325° oven until lightly browned. Serve warm or cold. The jelly and meringue may be omitted, and the pudding served with cream, or Chocolate or Lemon Sauce (Chapter VIII).

CARAMEL CUSTARD

A simple version of Crème Renversée, delicate and very easy to make.

> 3 eggs
> ¼ cup sugar
> ⅛ teaspoon salt
> 2 cups milk
> ½ teaspoon vanilla
> ¾ cup brown sugar

Beat the eggs with a wire whisk until light and fluffy. Add the sugar and salt, mix well. Scald the milk and pour it slowly into the egg mixture, stirring constantly. Add the vanilla. Sift the brown sugar into the bottom of a buttered mold or casserole and carefully pour the custard on top of it. Set the mold in a shallow pan of hot water and bake in a 325° oven for about an hour, or until a silver knife inserted in the center comes out clean. Cool and invert on a serving platter. The brown sugar will have formed a caramel sauce.

AUGUST'S FLOWER
The Poppy

CHOCOLATE CORNSTARCH PUDDING

    4½ tablespoons cornstarch
    ⅔ cup sugar
    ⅛ teaspoon salt
    3 ounces chopped, unsweetened chocolate
    3 cups milk
    1 teaspoon vanilla
    2 tablespoons butter

Combine the cornstarch, sugar, salt and chopped chocolate in the top of a double boiler and mix well. Slowly stir in milk. Place over boiling water and stir with a whisk until thick and smooth, and chocolate is well-blended. Cook a few minutes longer. Remove from heat, add butter, cool and add vanilla. Pour into dessert dishes and serve with cream or whipped cream.

BUTTERSCOTCH PUDDING

Follow the directions for Chocolate Cornstarch Pudding, but substitute ¾ cup packed brown sugar for the white sugar, omit the chocolate and increase the butter to 3 tablespoons. Serve with cream or whipped cream and a sprinkling of chopped toasted nuts.

VANILLA CORNSTARCH PUDDING
(*Blanc Mange*)

A simple and delicious ending to a family dinner.

    3 cups milk
    4 tablespoons sugar
    ¼ teaspoon salt
    ¼ cup cornstarch
    1 egg
    ½ teaspoon vanilla

Combine 2 tablespoons of the sugar with the salt and cornstarch in a bowl. Mix well. Add ¾ cup of the milk

SEPTEMBER'S FLOWER
The Morning Glory

and blend. Meanwhile, scald the remaining 2¼ cups of milk in the top of a double boiler. Add the first mixture to the hot milk, mix well, and cook over hot water, stirring constantly until thick.

Beat the egg with the remaining 2 tablespoons of sugar until light. Pour a little of the hot mixture into the beaten egg mixture, blend, then pour the egg mixture back into the top of the double boiler. Stir and cook about 2 minutes more, remove from heat and cool. Add vanilla. Pour into glass dessert dishes and chill. Serve plain or with a little whipped cream or crushed fruit. Or serve with Butterscotch Sauce, Chocolate Sauce or Sauce Melba (Chapter VIII).

ORANGE PUDDING CAKE (*Sponge Custard*)

This custard is called a "pudding cake," because during baking the batter separates, leaving a spongy cake-like top and a sauce-like substance at the bottom.

> 1½ tablespoons butter
> ¾ cup sugar
> 1 tablespoon grated orange rind
> 3 eggs, separated
> 3 tablespoons sifted flour
> ⅓ cup fresh orange juice
> 1 cup milk
> ⅛ teaspoon salt

Cream the butter, gradually add the sugar and orange rind, cream again. Add the egg yolks, one at a time, and beat well after each addition. Stir in the flour alternately with the orange juice and milk. Beat the egg whites with the salt until stiff and carefully fold into the yolk mixture. Pour into a 7″ buttered casserole and set in a shallow pan of hot water. Bake about 1 hour in a 350° oven until set. Serve warm or, even better, well-chilled with thick cream.

O CTOBER'S FLOWER
The Hop

N ovember's flower
The Chrysanthemum

COTTAGE PUDDING

This remains an old-fashioned and delightful favorite that can be varied according to the dessert sauce you serve with it.

> ¼ cup butter
> ½ cup sugar
> 1 egg
> 1½ cups sifted flour
> 2 teaspoons baking powder
> ¼ teaspoon salt
> ½ cup milk
> 1 teaspoon vanilla

Cream the butter till fluffy, add sugar a little at a time, and cream again. Beat in the egg. Combine the flour, baking powder and salt and sift again. Add the dry ingredients to the butter-sugar-egg mixture alternating with the milk a little at a time. Add vanilla. Stir until smooth. Pour into a buttered 8″ x 8″ pan. Bake at 350° about 30 minutes, or until done.

While very fresh, cut into squares and serve with Custard Sauce, Butterscotch Sauce, Chocolate Fudge or Bittersweet Sauce, Sauce Melba, Lemon Sauce (Chapter VIII) or crushed sweetened fruit.

BOSTON CREAM PIE
(*Sometimes called Washington Cream Pie*)

Bake the cake for Cottage Pudding in buttered 8″ layer pans at 375° for about 25 minutes. Cool and fill with a delicate custard filling. (See Crème Patissière, Chapter VIII.) Ice the top with ½ recipe Uncooked Chocolate Butter Icing (Chapter VIII).

D<small>ECEMBER'S FLOWER</small>
The Holly

SURPRISE CUPCAKES

These are the special joy of children and are very convenient to serve at picnics and large gatherings.

Bake the cake for Cottage Pudding in buttered muffin tins, filled ⅔ full. Bake for about 25 minutes in a 350° oven. After cooling, cut a thin slice from the top of each cupcake and fill with jam, English Lemon Curd (Chapter VIII), or sweetened whipped cream. Replace the tops and dust with confectioners' sugar or ice with any Uncooked Butter Icing (Chapter VIII).

You may also use the recipe for Chocolate Peppermint Cake, and then fill and ice the cakes as above. Choose filling and icing from Chapter VIII.

BANANA BREAD

A moist, fine-flavored "bread" that is rich enough to serve for dessert or tea, and fine for breakfast. Very simple to make.

```
    3  large ripe bananas (or 4 small ones)
    1  cup sugar
    1  egg
   ¼  cup butter, melted and cooled
    1  teaspoon baking soda
    1  teaspoon salt
1½  cups sifted flour
    1  scant teaspoon vanilla
   ¼  cup finely slivered almonds (optional)
```

Mash banana in a large mixing bowl with a fork or low speed electric mixer. Blend in sugar, butter and egg. Mix well. Sift together the baking soda, flour and salt and blend with the first mixture. Add vanilla and almonds. Pour into a buttered loaf pan, 8½″ x 4½″ and bake in a 325° oven for 50 to 60 minutes.

T wo plum-puddings
are better than one.
OLD MAXIM

APPLE CRISP

A fine-tasting dessert whose flavor depends on the quality of the apples.

APPLE LAYER

> 4 cups peeled, cored and sliced tart
>   cooking apples
> ½ cup sugar (or to taste)
> ½ teaspoon cinnamon
> ½ teaspoon nutmeg

Gently mix the apples with the other ingredients and put into an ovenproof casserole about 7″ in diameter.

TOPPING

> ¼ cup brown sugar
> ¼ teaspoon salt
> ½ cup sifted flour
> ½ cup dry oatmeal
> ¼ cup butter
> ½ cup chopped nuts

Mix the sugar, salt, flour and oatmeal in a bowl. Cut in the butter with a pastry blender, just until blended. Stir in the nuts and spread evenly over the apples. Bake in a 375° oven about ½ hour, or until apples are tender. Serve warm or cold with cream.

GINGERBREAD

Hot gingerbread served with plenty of butter makes a fine dessert. Or you may prefer it with cream or vanilla ice cream.

> ½ cup butter
> 1 cup brown sugar
> 2 eggs
> 2 cups sifted flour

1 teaspoon cinnamon
1 teaspoon baking soda
½ teaspoon salt
1½ teaspoons ginger
½ cup boiling water
½ cup dark molasses

Cream the butter till fluffy, add sugar and cream again. Beat in the eggs, one at a time. Mix the flour, cinnamon, soda, salt and ginger and resift. Stir together the boiling water and molasses. Add to the butter-egg mixture alternately with the dry ingredients. Mix well. Pour into a buttered 8″ x 10″ pan and bake at 350° about 40 minutes or until done.

BAKED APPLES

A perennial favorite, second in the eyes of apple lovers only to apple pie.

6 medium-sized baking apples
12 tablespoons brown sugar
6 teaspoons butter
cinnamon

Wash and core the apples, without cutting through the stem ends. Pare the skin from the upper fourth of each. Place in a baking dish and fill the centers with brown sugar, using two tablespoons for each apple. Dot with butter and sprinkle with cinnamon. Cover the bottom of the dish with boiling water and bake in a 375° oven for about 40 minutes, or until tender. Baste the apples frequently as they bake.

The apples will be even more appealing glazed. To glaze apples, sprinkle with granulated sugar after they have been baked. Run under the broiler until the sugar melts. Serve with cream.

CHAPTER VI

ESPECIALLY SOPHISTICATED

Wine, Cheese and Fruit

In Europe, the combination of fruit, cheese and wine has for generations been enthusiastically accepted as a noteworthy dessert—one that usually provides for a bit of pleasant ritual and always results in an artistic overall effect. Such acceptance is partly because all these "natural" products appeal pleasurably to a number of senses. But there is perhaps another and still more important reason: in taking the proper time to savor each sip of wine—fully appreciating its color and bouquet—with appropriate interludes taken for sampling *aged* cheese and *fresh* fruit—the period for good conversation is extended.

The leisurely enjoyment of fruit, cheese and wine is as easy to achieve in America as it is in Europe, particularly if you are willing to take that little extra time that goes with gracious living.

Five of the classic dessert wines served with fruit, cheese and Madeleines

WINE *is the intellectual part of a meal. Meats are merely the material part.*
ALEXANDER DUMAS

Taste in wine (as in cheese) is a matter of progressive development. Wine is a complex beverage, cheese a complex food. Accordingly, the subtle variations in taste are practically limitless. But how pleasant a learning process! The *classic* dessert wines and cheeses are relatively few, so here is a good place to start gathering knowledge that will widen your horizons in the art of good living.

For serving wines to their best advantage, choose an all-purpose glass that does the job admirably. Our favorite is a nicely-stemmed clear, tulip-shaped glass that is approximately 6 inches tall, with a bowl about 3½ inches deep. Such a bowl holds about 9 ounces and, when this is filled just a shade above half, the balance of the glass is excellent. Because the mouth of the glass is slightly smaller than the widest part of the bowl, the bouquet of the wine is captured for your continued enjoyment. The merit of the clear glass is evident: you sip wine rather than gulp it, and often you admire its matchless color. Except for champagne, such a glass sets off any wine.

GOOD COMPANIONS

As a workable rule of thumb, serve a light dry wine with lighter and more delicately-flavored cheeses; a fuller white or light red wine with cheeses in the middle range of flavors; and the fullest bodied of red wines with the strongest flavors.

The specific combinations of cheese and wine are many, particularly since many of the classic cheeses vary greatly in character with age, and accordingly are best complemented with different wines at different stages. Much flexibility in matching up wines and cheeses can be exercised, but keep in mind that *neither should dominate.* Just as a very brief guide, here are a few suggestions which are both sound and safe:

Especially Sophisticated

FROM *the mildest wine to the headiest and most perfumed: this is the right order of drinking.*
BRILLAT-SAVARIN

With delicate cheeses such as the rich double and triple crèmes or Hablé Crème Chantilly	Pouilly-Fuissé, Graves or a fine Rosé
With medium Port-Salut, well-aged cheddar or Camembert	Light Red Beaujolais ("the red wine of friendship") or light red Medoc
With Brie	Fuller-bodied and more matured Medoc
With aged Port-Salut, Livaro, Roquefort and other veined cheeses	Full-bodied red Burgundy, St. Emilion, Pomerol or Rhone
With Stilton, the favorite of the English	Port or cream sherry

The suggestions above assume the wines and cheeses follow a dinner in which the cuisine is basically French or middle-European. Suggestions for possible combinations following Italian cuisine might be:

Fontina d'Aosta, Bel Paese, Provolone or young Parmesan	Orvieto, Soave, Bardolino or Valpolicella
With Gorgonzola, Romano or aged Parmesan	Red Chianti, Bardolo, Barbera or Barbaresco

In serving wine with fresh fruits, one special word of caution should be remembered: be sure the wine is of very good quality, as any flaw, however small, will show up clearly when taken with fruit. While a rather wide variety of wines have in recent years been recommended as the ideal accompaniments to various fruits, most such suggestions as nectarines with cream sherry, tangerines with tokay and oranges with sau-

114

YOU'LL *have no
scandal while
you dine,
but honest talk
and wholesome wine.*
TENNYSON

ternes do not appeal to me. My suggestion is to avoid serving wine with such citrus fruits as grapefruit or orange and for such other fruits as grapes, raisins, apples, berries, peaches, melons and pears offer a Sauterne or Barsac.

As a snack, though usually not after a heavy meal, fruit torte or fruit cake might well be accompanied by Tokay or one of the Rhine wines ranging from Auslese to Beerenauslese, and a heavier cake or pastry might have such a companion wine as Port, Cream Sherry, Malmsey Madeira or Golden Marsala. No wine is recommended as a suitable complement to the flavors of chocolate or brandied fruits. Nor do I personally favor the use of wine as a beverage for dunking. One well-recognized wine expert does refer to the French custom of dunking madeleines, the specially-molded sponge cakes, in the remains of a distinguished Burgundy. The practice may be permissible, but—with no snobbishness intended—it is not for me. You, however, can be the ultimate judge.

Once you have taken the time to sample a few of the conversation-extending dessert wines, see if you don't think the late Ernest Hemingway gave this great beverage the proper praise when he said: "Wine is one of the civilized things in the world that has been brought to the greatest perfection, and it offers a greater range of enjoyment and appreciation than possibly any other purely sensory thing which may be purchased". Learn to suit a great wine to a great occasion and we believe it is safe to forecast that you will add something extra to your enjoyment of life!

SIG LANGSTADTER

Mr. Langstadter's early life was spent in one of the renowned wine districts of Bavaria, where he was for many years employed by a leading winery. Since becoming an American citizen, he has put his extensive knowledge of the wines of Europe and America to work as a wine consultant.

CHAPTER VII

REPERTOIRE OF BASICS

From these nine magic mixtures you can turn out flaky *Milles-Feuilles* cakes, a festive *Gâteau Grande Fête*, delicious tarts and tartlets, a towering *Croquembouche*, Perfect Lemon Pie and hundreds of other classic pastries. Some are surprisingly simple to make; others take a little time and practice to achieve perfection.

Use the best ingredients you can buy . . . sweet butter (if lightly salted omit salt in the recipe), the freshest large eggs and pure flavoring extracts. The flour in these recipes is the regular all-purpose flour. Sift it first, then lightly spoon into a measuring cup and level with a knife.

The oven is your most important tool. Preheat for 15 minutes before starting to bake. Test the accuracy of the oven thermometer by checking with another thermometer, and adjust the heat accordingly. And *be sure* not to overload the oven, since nothing will then bake perfectly.

If you'd like to achieve a reputation for being at all times prepared to serve a spectacular company dessert, bake some of these basics at your convenience ahead of time, on a rainy day or during a free evening. Wrap the cakes or pastries well and freeze them. Then you'll be ready to add the final touches of sauce, filling or icing in just a few minutes.

PASTRY FOR PIES

A perfect tender pie crust can be achieved by keeping in mind 3 prohibitions: don't use too much flour, or the crust will be tough; don't use too much shortening or it will be crumbly; and don't use too much water, or it will be heavy. On the positive side, have all the ingredients as cold as possible. This will make a 9″ 2-crust pie.

2 cups sifted flour	**¼ cup ice water**
1 teaspoon salt	**1 cup vegetable shortening**

Mix the flour with the salt and sift into a large bowl. Cut two thirds of the shortening into the flour with a pastry blender till it is the consistency of corn meal. Cut the remaining third of the shortening until the particles are the size of large peas. Sprinkle with water and blend lightly with a fork until it just holds together in a ball. Wrap in wax paper and chill for half an hour or more. (It will keep for days in the refrigerator.)

Roll the chilled dough between sheets of waxed paper, lifting the rolling pin at the end of each stroke. Trim it in a circle one inch larger than the pan. Fold in half and lay the fold across the center of the pan. Then unfold. Fit it loosely into the pan, and make a crimped edge with your thumb and forefinger for a one-crust pie. If you are making a two crust pie, allow the lower crust to hang over the edge of the pan slightly, add filling and cover with the top crust, cut to size. Bring the edges of the lower crust over the top crust and fold it over like a hem. Press edges with a fork, or flute with your fingers.

TIME TABLE FOR BAKING PIES:
(*be sure oven is pre-heated*)

2 crust fruit pies	*450° for 10 minutes, 350° for additional 35 or more minutes*
2 crust mince pie	*450° for 30 minutes*
Pie shells, without fillings	*450° for 15 to 20 minutes*
Pumpkin and most other one-crust pies with uncooked filling	*450° for 15 minutes 325° for additional 30 minutes*

PUFF PASTE (*Pâté Feuilletée*)

This is the flaky, many-layered pastry that is the glory of European baking and the basis of many of its most lavish desserts. Its production is time-consuming, but well within the range of any careful cook. Anyone who has ever eaten puff pastry at its freshly-baked best will say it is well worth the trouble.

It was probably the ancient Persians who first made *feuilletée* and passed the recipe to the Greeks. The pastry is mentioned in a charter written by Robert, bishop of Amiens, in 1311. It is believed the recipe was simplified in the seventeenth century by Claude Lorrain, who was a *patissier* before he turned landscape painter.

The best puff paste is made from bread flour (sometimes obtainable at bakeries) because it has the high gluten content that helps to achieve the many thin layers that will not collapse during baking. However, regular all-purpose flour can be used.

The following recipe will make 50 *Papillons,* or a large *Mille-Feuilles* cake. You may keep well-wrapped puff paste in the refrigerator 3 or 4 days, or it can be formed into shapes and frozen, to be baked as long as three months later.

> **4 cups sifted flour**
> **1 teaspoon salt**
> **1⅓ cups ice water**
> **1 pound (4 sticks) butter, preferably unsalted**

Sift the flour with the salt into a large bowl. Slowly add the ice water, mixing with a fork. Scrape out onto a floured board, and knead lightly just long enough to form into a ball. Cover the dough and put in the refrigerator about 10 minutes.

Take from refrigerator and shape into a 3 x 6″ rectangle with your hands, on a well-floured board. Roll out into a neat rectangle about 8 x 14″.

Lightly mark the center of the rectangle and lay the 4 sticks of butter on half of it, keeping them about 1½″ away from the 3 edges. (Butter should have been refrigerated until this time.) Fold the other half of the dough over the butter and pinch the edges together firmly to seal. Wrap in a piece of floured foil and refrigerate 30 minutes.

Put the chilled dough on a well floured board, pound with a rolling pin to distribute the butter. (Note the position of dough.) Refrigerate for 30 minutes.

Next roll out dough into a rectangle 8″ x 18″, uniformly thick. Do not roll over

118

ends. Fold top and bottom ends over center third of dough, making 3 layers. Wrap in floured foil and refrigerate 30 minutes.

Repeat this process 5 more times for a total of 6 rollings and 6 "rests" in the refrigerator. Always start to roll the dough with the narrow end toward you. The repeated rollings distribute the butter and make the many paper-thin layers.

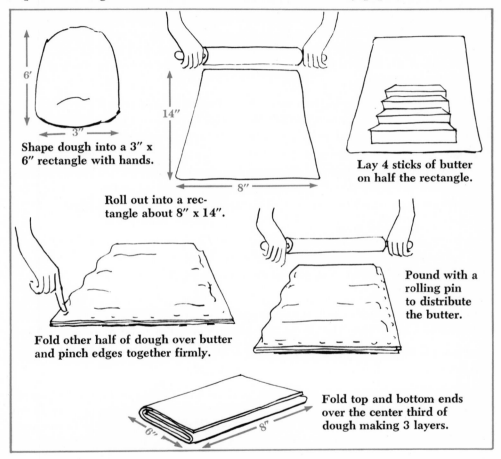

Shape dough into a 3" x 6" rectangle with hands.

Roll out into a rectangle about 8" x 14".

Lay 4 sticks of butter on half the rectangle.

Fold other half of dough over butter and pinch edges together firmly.

Pound with a rolling pin to distribute the butter.

Fold top and bottom ends over the center third of dough making 3 layers.

Store the dough in the refrigerator for at least 3 hours before final rolling. The thickness and shape you make the dough depends on what recipe you are making. Always cut the rolled dough with a very sharp knife to form the desired shape, and do not touch the cut edges with your fingers.

MERINGUE SUISSE *(Swiss meringue)*

This mixture is used for such delightful desserts as *Vacharin Chantilly,* and *Spanische Windtorte.* It can also be shaped into individual meringue shells, or cookies.

> **5 egg whites** (at room temperature)
> **¼ teaspoon cream of tartar**
> **¼ teaspoon salt**
> **1 teaspoon vanilla**
> **1¼ cups sugar**

The secret of crisp tender meringues is in the baking—they should be dried, rather than baked, so they become just the palest off white, and do not become tough. Set the oven at 200° *before* beating the egg whites.

Put the egg whites, cream of tartar, vanilla and salt in a large bowl and beat at medium speed with an electric mixer until the mixture holds soft peaks. Add one half the sugar, (a tablespoon at a time, as you continue beating). Continue beating until the meringue is stiff and dull, and until a bit rubbed between the fingers is smooth, *not* grainy. It should be stiff enough to hold its shape when formed with a pastry tube. Fold in the remaining sugar.

Form the meringue as directed for the particular recipe on a well-buttered, lightly-floured baking sheet. Put in the preheated oven for 15 minutes. Then turn off the heat and allow the meringue to stay in the oven for at least 4 or 5 hours—overnight is better.

If time is a factor, do the second best thing and bake meringue layers at 200° for about 40 minutes, small meringues a few minutes less.

They can be stored in a dry, airy place (*not* tightly covered) for several weeks.

SWISS BROYAGE

Similar in texture to meringue, but a little less sweet and more flavorful, because of the ground nuts. Broyage is delicious by itself but is usually used in combination with other cakes. Spread with butter-cream and stored in the refrigerator for a day or two it will mellow and soften.

> **3 egg whites (at room temperature)**
> **1 teaspoon vanilla**
> **⅛ teaspoon cream of tartar**
> **dash of salt**
> **¾ cup of sugar**
> **⅓ cup sifted cornstarch**
> **¼ cup blanched almonds, ground or finely grated**

Combine egg whites, cream of tartar, salt and vanilla in a large bowl. Beat with an electric mixer at medium speed until soft peaks form. Add ½ cup of sugar, a tablespoon at a time, beating constantly until mixture is dull and firm enough to force through a pastry tube. Combine the almonds, cornstarch and remaining sugar and fold into the egg-white mixture.

Form the Broyage as the particular recipe for which it is being used directs. Use the same method of baking as for Meringue Suisse. Makes 2 thin 9″ layers or twenty-four 2″ cookies.

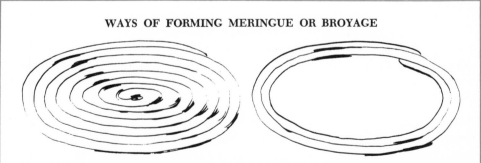

WAYS OF FORMING MERINGUE OR BROYAGE

Fit a pastry bag with a medium or large-size tube. Fill with meringue or broyage. Mark a circle by pressing a round pan lightly on a buttered and floured baking sheet. Press out a continuous spiral of the meringue or broyage, starting in center, to form a layer. Rings are made the same way, leaving center of circle empty.

PÂTÉ À CHOU (*Cream puff paste*)

This versatile mixture is the basis of many distinguished desserts. It is surprisingly simple to make for even the most inexperienced cook. For guaranteed foolproof results have all the ingredients at room temperature, and make sure of an accurate oven temperature.

> **1 cup water**
> **½ cup butter**
> **1 cup sifted flour**
> **¼ teaspoon salt**
> **4 eggs**

Put the water and butter in a saucepan and bring to a boil. Lower the heat, add the flour and salt all at once and continue to cook, stirring constantly until the mixture leaves the sides of the pan and forms a ball.

Remove from the heat and add the eggs, one at a time, making sure each egg is well-blended before adding the next.

This amount will make 12 large cream puffs or éclairs, or 36 to 40 *profiteroles*.

TO FORM AND BAKE CREAM PUFFS

Butter a cookie sheet. Fit a pastry bag with a large plain tube and press out high mounds of the paste about 1½″ in diameter. Allow 2″ between the mounds for spreading. Bake at 400° for 30 minutes until puffs are golden and no beads of moisture show. Reduce heat to 350° and bake 5 or 10 minutes longer. Remove from oven, put on rack and with a sharp knife make a gash in the side of each puff to allow steam to escape.

Éclairs are formed the same way, pressing the paste into a slender pencil shape about 3″ long. Lacking a pastry bag, the puffs or éclairs may be formed with spoons.

TO FORM PROFITEROLES (TINY CREAM PUFFS)

Use a medium size tube. Bake in a 400° oven for 20 to 25 minutes until puffed and golden and no beads of moisture show. Turn off heat and leave the puffs in a closed oven for 10 minutes more.

RICH TART PASTRY (*Wiener Murbteig*)

This is the crisp, delicious pastry that is the base for subtly-flavored European tarts, tarlets and barquettes. The cook who has mastered the art of making tart pastry will find it easy to turn out many spectacular desserts, so it is a worthwhile project to practice on until perfect. This recipe will make two 8-inch tart shells or more than a dozen small tarts or barquettes.

3 cups sifted flour	3 eggs
¾ cup sugar	½ teaspoon vanilla or
⅛ teaspoon salt	2 teaspoons grated lemon rind
¼ cup butter, firm but not hard	

Mix the flour with the sugar and salt and sift it onto a mixing board, or into a large bowl. Make a well in the center and into it put the butter (cut in large flakes), the eggs and the vanilla or lemon rind. Make a paste of the ingredients with your finger tips, gradually working in the flour mixture, until a smooth firm dough is formed. Work quickly so the butter does not become oily. When the board (or sides of the bowl) is clean, wrap the dough in wax paper and chill until firm enough to roll.

Roll out the chilled dough between sheets of waxed paper to a thickness of less than ¼". Fit the dough carefully over the *outside* of the tart or tartlet pans, patting gently into shape. Prick all over with a fork. Some cooks prefer to line flan rings or tart pans with the dough, then fit a piece of foil into the tart shell and fill it with uncooked rice. The foil is left on for the first 10 minutes of baking, or until the tart is set, then lifted out and the dough pricked all over with a fork before finishing baking.

Whichever way you have formed the dough, freeze it for 1½ hours before baking.

Small barquette or tartlet shells are baked in a 350° oven (*on the middle shelf*) for about 10 or 12 minutes, or until golden. Filled tartlets are baked at the same 350° temperature on the *lowest* shelf of the oven for about 20 minutes.

Bake large unfilled tart shells *on the middle shelf* of the oven at 350° about 25 minutes. Bake filled tarts on the *lowest* shelf of a 350° oven about 40 minutes. Shaped tart pastry may be frozen for weeks, then baked, losing none of its flavor.

GÉNOISE (*Delicate butter sponge cake*)

6 eggs, separated
1 cup sugar
1 teaspoon vanilla
1 cup sifted flour
½ cup clarified butter, melted and cooled

Combine eggs, sugar and vanilla in a large bowl and stir till just combined. Set bowl over saucepan containing 1" or 2" hot water. (Water should not touch bottom of bowl.) Place over very low heat for 5 or 10 minutes, or until eggs are just lukewarm. Stir mixture several times to prevent it from cooking at the bottom of the bowl.

When mixture feels lukewarm and looks like a bright yellow syrup, remove from heat and beat at high speed for 10 or 15 minutes, or until it has tripled in volume and draws out in ribbon form when a spoon is pulled out of it.

Sprinkle the flour, a little at a time, on top of the whipped mixture. Fold in very gently. Then fold in the butter. *Do not over mix.*

Pour the batter into well-buttered pans, dusted lightly with flour, and bake at 350° for about 25 minutes, or until cake pulls away from sides of pan. Remove from pans immediately and cool on rack.

Makes two 9" layers, three 7" layers or one 11" x 16" sheet.

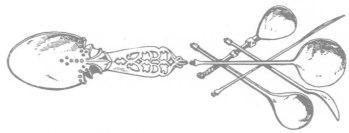

HOW TO CLARIFY BUTTER

Place any quantity of butter in a deep pan. Melt over very low heat and continue cooking until the foam disappears from the top. The liquid butter must not brown. When the butter looks perfectly clear, remove from heat and pour through a sieve lined with cheesecloth into a container, leaving sediment in the pan. (If only a small amount is being made, simply pour off the clear butter, leaving the sediment in the pan.)

Clarified butter, well covered, will keep for months in the refrigerator. It is pure fat from which all solids and water have been removed.

ALMOND CAKE

¾ cup sifted flour
¼ cup clarified butter, melted and cooled (on opposite page)
3 eggs
2 egg yolks
½ teaspoon vanilla
½ cup sugar
1 teaspoon grated lemon rind
¼ cup almond paste

Combine the three eggs, one egg yolk, vanilla, sugar and lemon rind in a large bowl. Heat over hot water as in Génoise recipe (on opposite page). When the egg mixture is warm and looks like a bright yellow syrup, remove bowl from heat and beat until almost triple in bulk. Cream the almond paste with the remaining egg yolk until fluffy.

Pour the almond paste mixture over the beaten egg mixture. Sprinkle the flour on top. Fold gently together, pouring in the butter as you fold, with a wooden spoon or with electric mixer at lowest speed. *Do not over mix.*

Butter an 11 x 16″ jelly roll pan, line the bottom with wax paper and butter again. Spread batter in pan and bake at 350° about 15 minutes, or until golden and shrunk from sides of pan. Or use a 9″ layer cake pan prepared in the same way and bake 20 to 25 minutes, or until done.

BASIC SPONGE SHEET

6 eggs, separated   1 teaspoon vanilla
¼ teaspoon salt   ½ cup flour
½ cup sugar

Beat the egg whites with the salt until they stand in soft peaks. Add 4 tablespoons of the sugar, one tablespoon at a time, and continue beating until meringue is very stiff. In a separate bowl beat the egg yolks with the remaining sugar and vanilla until fluffy.

Gently fold about one-fourth of the meringue into the egg yolk mixture. Then pour back into the bowl of meringue. Sprinkle with 2 tablespoons of the flour and fold together. Repeat until all the flour is blended. Be careful not to over-mix.

Pour into a buttered 11″ x 16″ jelly roll pan that has been lined with buttered wax paper. Bake 10 to 12 minutes in a 400° oven until golden. Remove from pan immediately to cool on a rack. (See Bûche de Noël, Lincoln Log for directions for rolling.)

CHOCOLATE SPONGE SHEET

Follow the recipe for Basic Sponge Sheet, but substitute ¼ cup of dark sifted cocoa for ¼ cup of the flour. Sift the flour and cocoa together before adding to the batter.

CHAPTER VIII

ICINGS, FILLINGS
AND SAUCES

Final touches   *with a flair*

Classic desserts were created by artist-chefs, but this does not mean their recipes are rigid and inflexible. Just as the director of a symphony orchestra puts his stamp on the music he conducts, so too can you be a creative *patissier* by using these delicious final touches to achieve your interpretation of the classic.

While the impressive *croquembouche* is always identifiable, no two master chefs would ever produce identical twins of this famous cream puff tower. There are also probably as many versions of *Vacherin Chantilly* as there are *patissiers*. Every tray of tiny cream puffs or *petits fours* presents a real artistic challenge in choosing flavors and tints in fillings and icings. And even the great Escoffier found a way to improve his original Pêches Melba!

To make many of these desserts masterpieces look as appealing as they taste, skill with a pastry bag and tube is important. A little practice will soon develop the technique you need to turn out a *Charlotte Russe* as tempting as Carême's.

CONTINENTAL BUTTER CREAM

A smooth, rich concoction used for both filling and frosting continental cakes.

⅔ cup sugar
⅓ cup water
⅛ teaspoon cream of tartar
5 egg yolks
1 cup soft butter

Mix sugar, water and cream of tartar in a saucepan. Stir over low heat until sugar is completely dissolved. Raise heat and boil without stirring until syrup tests 238°.

Meanwhile, beat the egg yolks in a bowl until they are fluffy. Then pour the hot syrup in a thin stream into the yolks, beating constantly. The mixture will become thick and light as it cools from the beating. Set aside until completely cooled. Beat in softened butter, a little at a time. Flavor to your taste.

Makes 2 cups. Butter cream may be kept in the refrigerator for a week or two.

CHOCOLATE BUTTER CREAM

Beat 3 ounces melted, unsweetened chocolate and 3 tablespoons of cognac into 2 cups of Butter Cream.

MOCHA BUTTER CREAM

Beat 5 ounces of melted, semi-sweet chocolate, 4 tablespoons of extra strong coffee and 3 tablespoons of cognac into 2 cups of Butter Cream.

SEVEN MINUTE ICING

A very fluffy white icing that never fails.

2 egg whites
1½ cups sugar
5 tablespoons cold water
¼ teaspoon cream of tartar
1 teaspoon vanilla

Place all the ingredients except vanilla in the top of a double boiler and beat with a whisk or electric beater until well-blended. Then place over rapidly boiling water and continue to beat for 7 minutes.

Remove from heat, add vanilla and continue to beat until the icing reaches the correct consistency to spread. Instead of the vanilla, you may flavor the icing with a few drops of oil of peppermint.

WILTON FONDANT

This icing is not easy to make, but it is perfect for icing cakes and essential for petits fours. It has a fine shiny finish.

> **3 cups sugar**
> **1½ cups water**
> **1 tablespoon white corn syrup**
> **⅛ teaspoon cream of tartar**

Combine all ingredients in a large, heavy saucepan. Heat slowly, stirring constantly until all the sugar is dissolved. When the syrup looks clear, wash down the sides of the pan with a brush dipped in cold water to remove any clinging sugar crystals. Without stirring, increase the heat and boil until it reaches 238° on a candy thermometer. Now pour onto a marble slab, porcelain table top or large metal platter.

When the mixture is lukewarm, stir briskly with a wooden spoon and work it toward the center until it begins to stiffen and look creamy. Then knead it until soft and pliable and has been worked into a smooth white ball. Store in a covered container for 24 hours to ripen before using. Tightly covered, it will keep at room temperature for several weeks.

USING FONDANT

Cakes iced with fondant should first be brushed with hot apricot glaze to seal the pores of the cake and help the icing stay shiny. Allow the glaze to dry.

Put about a cup of the ripened fondant into a heavy pan. Add a tablespoon or more of liquid (water, liqueur, orange or lemon juice or coffee). Add vanilla or other flavoring at this time. Warm over low heat, stirring constantly until creamy and barely lukewarm. It should be thick enough to mask the cake, but soft enough to pour and spread by itself. Do not overheat or it will lose its shine.

Place the petits fours or cake on a wire rack and pour the fondant over them. Work it quickly and keep a spatula handy to touch up any bare spots.

If you wish to tint the fondant, add the food color while fondant is warming.

CHOCOLATE FONDANT

Add 1 ounce melted, unsweetened chocolate and 1 teaspoon vanilla while the fondant is being warmed.

Puff pastry in variety—on the plate, a Napoleon

CONFECTIONERS' SUGAR GLAZES

These semi-liquid mixtures are designed to pour over Pound, Angel Food or Sponge cakes. Mix them as soon as the cake is put into the oven, and let them stand in a warm place while the cake bakes. The warmth will mellow the flavor.

LEMON GLAZE
Add the juice and grated rind of one lemon to one cup of sifted confectioners' sugar. Mix well, warm and pour over cake.

ORANGE GLAZE
Add ⅓ cup orange juice, one teaspoon lemon juice and the grated rind of one orange to one cup sifted confectioners' sugar. Mix well, warm and pour over cake.

VANILLA GLAZE
Add ⅓ cup milk and 1 teaspoon vanilla to 1 cup sifted confectioners' sugar. Mix well, warm and pour over cake.

FRUIT GLAZES

APRICOT GLAZE FOR TARTS MADE WITH LIGHT-COLORED FRUITS
Put one cup of Apricot Jam through a sieve and heat to boiling. Remove from heat and stir in two to four tablespoons of cognac, kirsch or other liqueur. Use while hot. This is also used for glazing cakes before icing.

CURRANT GLAZE FOR TARTS MADE WITH RED FRUITS
Put one cup of Currant Jelly through a sieve and heat to boiling. Remove from heat and stir in two to four tablespoons of kirsch. Use while hot.

WILTON BUTTERCREAM ICING

A fine icing both for icing the cake and for decorating with a pastry bag and tube. *The* icing for birthday cakes!

⅔ cup white vegetable shortening	¼ cup cream
⅓ cup soft butter	1 teaspoon vanilla
1½ cups confectioners' sugar	⅛ teaspoon salt

Cream the shortening and butter, add the sugar a little at a time and cream again. Slowly add the cream, then the salt and vanilla. Beat with an electric mixer at high speed for 5 minutes.

The icing may be stored in a covered container in the refrigerator, then brought to room temperature and whipped again before using. You may tint it with food color and vary the flavoring to your taste. Thin it with a few drops of water for piping script messages on cakes. Flowers made with this icing should be placed in the refrigerator to harden before positioning on cake.

UNCOOKED BUTTER ICING

The following uncooked icings are delicious and easy to make and use. To counter-act the slightly raw taste that may be present, allow the finished icing to rest in a bowl in a warm place as the cake is baking, then beat again before spreading on the cake.

> ½ cup soft butter
> 1 pound sifted confectioners' sugar
> ⅛ teaspoon salt
> 4 to 5 tablespoons cream
> 1½ teaspoons vanilla

Cream the butter till fluffy, add sugar gradually, beating till blended. Add salt. Stir in cream, a little at a time, using just enough to give a good spreading consistency. Add vanilla.

Makes enough to frost top and sides of two 9″ layers, or 24 cup cakes.

UNCOOKED LEMON ICING

Substitute lemon juice for the cream in Uncooked Butter Icing and add the grated rind of 1 lemon instead of the vanilla.

UNCOOKED ORANGE ICING

Substitute 1 teaspoon lemon juice and 4 tablespoons orange juice for the cream in Uncooked Butter Icing and add the grated rind of 1 orange instead of the vanilla.

UNCOOKED BITTERSWEET CHOCOLATE ICING

> 4 ounces unsweetened chocolate
> 3 tablespoons hot water
> 1¼ cups sifted confectioners' sugar
> 1 egg
> ¼ cup soft butter
> 1 teaspoon vanilla

Melt chocolate in the top of a double boiler, add hot water and stir until smooth. Remove from the heat and blend in the sugar. Add egg and beat until smooth. Add butter, a little at a time, beating well after each addition. Stir in vanilla.

Makes enough icing for two 9″ layers, or 24 cupcakes.

Substitute 3 tablespoons strong, freshly-brewed coffee for the hot water in Uncooked Bittersweet Chocolate Icing and omit the vanilla.

UNCOOKED CHOCOLATE BUTTER ICING
Follow the recipe for Uncooked Bittersweet Chocolate Icing, but use only 2 ounces of unsweetened chocolate, and increase the confectioners' sugar to about 1¾ cups.

COCONUT PECAN ICING

This is the icing that adds so much to German Sweet Chocolate Cake.

> 1 cup sweetened evaporated milk
> 3 egg yolks
> 1 teaspoon vanilla
> 1⅓ cups shredded coconut
> 1 cup coarsely chopped pecans

Combine the milk, egg yolks and butter in a heavy saucepan and cook over medium heat, stirring constantly until thickened (about 12 minutes). Remove from heat, stir in vanilla, coconut and pecans, and beat to spreading consistency. Fills and frosts the top of a 9″ two-layer cake.

CARAMEL ICING

> ½ cup butter
> 2½ tablespoons flour
> ¼ teaspoon salt
> ½ cup milk
> ½ cup brown sugar, packed
> 2 cups sifted confectioners' sugar
> ½ teaspoon vanilla
> ½ cup chopped walnuts

Melt butter, remove from heat, blend in flour and salt, slowly stir in milk. Bring to boil, stirring constantly. (It will curdle—don't be alarmed.) Boil 1 minute. Stir in brown sugar, remove from heat, and stir in confectioners' sugar. Set in pan of cold water and beat until right consistency to spread. Add vanilla and walnuts.

CRÈME PÂTISSIÈRE *(Pastry Cream)*
A rich, delicate filling for continental cakes and tarts.

> 3 tablespoons flour
> ⅛ teaspoon salt
> ⅜ cup sugar
> 1 cup light cream
> 4 egg yolks (slightly beaten)
> 1 teaspoon vanilla or
>   1″ piece of vanilla bean

Mix the flour, salt and sugar in a heavy saucepan, blend in a little of the cream and place on medium heat, stirring constantly. Add the rest of the cream and the vanilla or vanilla bean and continue stirring until the mixture becomes as thick as a medium cream sauce.

Stir a little of the heated sauce into the egg yolks, then pour the egg yolks into the sugar-flour-cream mixture. Return to low heat and cook for a few more minutes till thickened. Do not let the sauce boil. Discard the vanilla bean (if used) and cool as quickly as possible. If vanilla bean was not used, add vanilla after removing from heat.

To prevent a skin from forming over the cream, brush with melted butter. Stir briefly before using.

Fills a 9″ tart shell or about a dozen small tartlet shells.

CRÈME PLOMBIÈRES
This is a light, velvety filling of a wonderful consistency and flavor.

> 1 ounce gelatin
> ¼ cup cold water
> 1 recipe Crème Patissière
> 1 cup heavy cream, whipped
> 2 tablespoons cognac

Put the water in a metal or pyrex cup, add the gelatin and heat in a small pan of boiling water till clear. (It is not necessary to stir.) Stir into the Crème Patissière. Fold the cognac into the whipped cream. Gently fold the two mixtures together.

Other Liqueurs may be substituted for cognac.

CRÈME ST. HONORÉ

  1 recipe Crème Patissière
  1 ounce gelatin
  ¼ cup cold water
  6 egg whites beaten stiff with a pinch of salt.

Put the water in a metal or pyrex cup and pour the gelatin over it. Set the cup in a small pan of boiling water and heat until the contents are clear. (It is not necessary to stir.) Stir thoroughly into the cool Crème Patissière. Fold the egg whites carefully into the mixture. Chill.

CRÈME AU CHOCOLAT

Make Crème Patissière. After removing from the heat add 2 ounces of melted, unsweetened chocolate to the mixture, along with the vanilla (if vanilla bean has not been used).

CRÈME ANGLAISE AU MOKA

Follow the recipe for Crème Patissière, but reduce the amount of light cream by 2 tablespoons, substituting 2 tablespoons extra-strong, freshly-brewed coffee.

CUSTARD SAUCE *(English Boiled Custard)*

This is the sauce about which Count Carrocioli, Napoleon's ambassador to London, remarked: "There are in England sixty different religions, and only one sauce". The English serve it over every variety of dessert pudding, and even mince pie! It is good, hot or cold.

  3 egg yolks   ⅛ teaspoon salt
  2 cups milk   1 teaspoon rosewater (optional)
  2 tablespoons sugar   1 teaspoon vanilla

Beat the egg yolks lightly with a fork in the top of a double boiler. Mix the milk with the sugar and salt and scald. Pour the hot milk mixture over the egg yolks, stirring constantly with a whisk. Place over simmering water and cook and stir for about 7 minutes, or until the mixture coats a spoon. Add the rosewater and vanilla. Pour into a serving bowl or pitcher.

FRANGIPANE CREAM

Legend has it that this almond-flavored filling was invented by Count Cesare Frangipani, a suitor of Catherine de Medici.

> **1 recipe Crème Patssière (page 134)**
> **¼ cup butter**
> **⅔ cup crumbled macaroons**
> **⅓ cup ground toasted almonds**

Stir in the butter, little by little, after the Crème Patisière has been taken from the heat and is still hot. Add the macaroons and almonds and cool.

PRALINE CREAM

A delectable filling for cream puffs, éclairs or *Paris-Brest*.

> **1 tablespoon lemon juice**
> **1 cup sugar**
> **½ cup toasted slivered or coarsely-**
> **chopped blanched almonds**
> **2 cups heavy cream, whipped**
> **2 teaspoons confectioners' sugar**

Mix the lemon juice and sugar in a heavy saucepan. Stirring constantly, heat until the syrup turns amber and is completely dissolved. Quickly stir in almonds and pour out on a well-buttered platter.

When this candy has cooled and hardened, break into pieces and grate with a nut grinder. Or put between sheets of wax paper and pound with a wooden potato masher. Whip the cream with the confectioners' sugar until stiff, and fold in the grated praline candy.

ENGLISH LEMON CURD

A fine filling for tarts or cakes.

> **5 egg yolks**
> **½ cup sugar**
> **2 large lemons (juice and grated rind)**
> **¼ cup butter**

Grate the lemon peel, and then squeeze out the juice and strain. Combine egg yolks and sugar in the top of a double boiler. Add lemon juice and grated peel, then butter little by little. Stir constantly until thick. This will keep in a covered jar in the refrigerator for months.

HOT RUM SAUCE

1 cup sugar
1 cup water
½ cup soft butter
¼ cup rum

Boil the sugar and water together until the syrup reaches the thread stage, 230°. Remove from heat, stir in the butter and, when that has melted, the rum. Serve immediately over mince pie or plum pudding. Wonderful!

BRANDY HARD SAUCE

½ cup butter
1½ cups confectioners' sugar
2 tablespoons brandy (or more, to taste)

Cream the butter until light and fluffy and gradually beat in the sugar. Add the brandy, still beating. Chill before serving. You may make rosettes of the hard sauce, using a pastry tube, before chilling.

BUTTERSCOTCH SAUCE

1 cup brown sugar, packed
⅓ cup melted butter
⅓ cup heavy cream

Blend the ingredients together in a heavy saucepan, bring to a boil and let it boil 5 minutes without stirring. Remove from the heat and beat for 30 seconds, or until foamy. Serve warm.

CHOCOLATE FUDGE SAUCE

1½ ounces unsweetened chocolate
1 tablespoon butter
2 tablespoons corn syrup
½ cup boiling water
1 cup sugar
⅛ teaspoon salt
½ teaspoon vanilla

Melt the chocolate over very low heat in a heavy saucepan. Add the other ingredients, except vanilla, stirring constantly. Increase heat and bring to a boil. Allow to boil three minutes. Cool slightly and stir in the vanilla. Delicious, hot or cold.

BITTERSWEET CHOCOLATE SAUCE

Follow the recipe for Chocolate Fudge Sauce (page 137), but use 3 ounces unsweetened chocolate instead of 1½ ounces.

MOCHA RUM SAUCE

> ½ cup strong coffee, freshly brewed
> 6 ounces dark sweet chocolate
> ½ ounce bitter chocolate
> 1 tablespoon rum

Cut the chocolate in small pieces and put in a heavy saucepan with the coffee. Cook over low heat, stirring constantly until the chocolate melts. Remove from heat, add the rum and stir until smooth. Serve hot.

SABAYON GLACÉ AU KIRSCH

> 6 egg yolks
> ¾ cup sugar
> ¾ cup marsala
> 2 tablespoons kirsch or rum
> 1 cup heavy cream, whipped (optional)

Beat together egg yolks and sugar in the top of a double boiler until light and pale in color. Stir in the wine and cook over hot, but not boiling water, whipping constantly until the mixture is thickened. Remove from heat; stir in the kirsch or rum, and continue to whip until cool. Chill the sauce and just before serving, fold in the whipped cream. Serve over mousse, pudding or fresh strawberries.

SAUCE MELBA *(Raspberry Purée)*

> 1 pint fresh raspberries
> 8-ounce jar currant jelly

Wash the raspberries and force through a sieve. Squeeze the jelly through a cheesecloth. Blend the two thoroughly and chill.

SAUCE MELBA II

In the event fresh raspberries are not available, frozen may be substituted. Thaw one package of frozen raspberries and force through a sieve. Heat the purée with ½ cup currant jelly. Mix well and cool.

LEMON SAUCE

½ cup sugar
⅛ teaspoon salt
1 tablespoon cornstarch
1 cup water

2 tablespoons butter
1 tablespoon grated lemon rind
3 tablespoons lemon juice
3 or 4 drops yellow food coloring

Mix the sugar, salt and cornstarch in a small heavy saucepan. Gradually add the water, stirring constantly. Place over low heat and cook till thickened and clear, stirring slowly with a whisk. Remove from heat and add the remaining ingredients. Mix well. Serve hot or cold over cakes and puddings.

CARAMEL SYRUP

For *Croquembouche, Vacharin Chantilly* and other desserts.

1 cup sugar
¼ teaspoon cream of tarter
⅓ cup water

Mix all the ingredients in a heavy saucepan and heat until amber and tests 271° on a candy thermometer. When using the syrup, place the pan over a bowl of very hot water and work quickly, as it hardens rapidly.

WHIPPED CREAM SAUCES

The uses of whipped cream as a dessert sauce are so many and varied that the cook could have almost no other sauces in her repertoire and still produce any number of delectable desserts. Here are just a few of the delicious variations on a theme. (And don't forget—whipped cream serves as a filling, as well as a sauce, for cream puffs or éclairs, cake layers and puff paste confections.)

Cream for whipping should be as heavy as obtainable and should be at least 1 day old. Well-covered, it will keep in the refrigerator for a week. If your family and guests love desserts (and you love to make them), it is advisable to have heavy cream on hand always.

Before whipping, make sure the cream, bowl and beaters are all very cold, especially in warm weather. Use an electric mixer at high speed, or a rotary egg beater. Sugar and flavoring extracts should be beaten into the cream just as it begins to thicken. Liqueur, fruit or cocoa are folded in after the cream has been whipped.

CREME CHANTILLY
Add 2 tablespoons sugar and ½ teaspoon vanilla to 1 cup heavy cream, whipped.

CREME CHANTILLY FOR DECORATING

Add 1 teaspoon gelatin to 2 tablespoons cold water in a metal or pyrex cup. Set in a small pan of boiling water and heat until gelatin dissolves and looks clear. Do not stir. Beat this mixture into 1 cup heavy cream just as the cream begins to thicken. Sweeten and flavor the whipped cream as in Crème Chantilly. Chill.

After chilling, this cream may be piped through a pastry tube and bag to form rosettes and swirls. It will keep in the refrigerator for a day or two.

Rosettes made with this cream may be frozen on a cookie sheet, or other flat surface, then stored in a plastic bag and kept frozen for weeks to be used for decorating puddings, jellies, parfaits and other desserts. Do not thaw the rosettes before arranging them on the dessert. They will soften in just a few minutes.

WHIPPED CREAM WITH LIQUEUR

Fold in 2 to 4 tablespoons of liqueur (kirsch, rum, cointreau, brandy, crème de cacao or framboise) into 1 cup heavy cream, whipped with a few grains of salt.

CHOCOLATE WHIPPED CREAM

Add 2 tablespoons sifted, unsweetened cocoa to 1 recipe Crème Chantilly (page 139).

CREME AMANDINE

Add ½ teaspoon lemon extract, ½ teaspoon almond extract and 2 tablespoons shredded toasted almonds to 1 recipe Crème Chantilly (page 139).

CREME AU FRUITS

Add ¼ cup sieved ripe fruit—peaches, apricots or fresh berries—to 1 recipe Crème Chantilly (page 139).

NEW ORLEANS WHIPPED CREAM

Fold 4 tablespoons sugar, 4 tablespoons lemon juice and the grated rind of 1 lemon into 1 cup heavy cream, whipped.

LIST OF ILLUSTRATIONS

INDEX